D1433366

JUST OVER YONDER

Humphrey Phelps

JUST OVER YONDER

Illustrated by Richard Reid

MICHAEL JOSEPH

LONDON

First published in Great Britain by Michael Joseph Limited
52 Bedford Square, London WC1B 3EF
1977

© by Humphrey Phelps 1977

ISBN: 0 7181 1638 0

Photoset in Plantin eleven on thirteen point
by Saildean Limited
Printed in Great Britain by
Billing & Sons Limited,
Guildford, London and Worcester

To Felicity

'Happy the man whose wish and care
A few paternal acres bound,
Content to breathe his native air,
In his own ground.'

Alexander Pope

CHAPTER ONE

Introductions and Innovations

Molly worked for Mr Clutterbuck at Willow Farm, which was quite close to Suttridge Farm where I'd worked since leaving school. Molly had arrived as a member of the Women's Land Army during the last winter of the war. A town girl, she soon adapted to the new way of life and was now part of the Clutterbuck family and of Willow Farm. By chance, I'd met her the day she arrived there; dressed in broad-brimmed hat, short overcoat, green jersey, breeches and thick stockings, and carrying a kit-bag.

She was a year younger than I, of medium height, neither plump nor thin, a comely girl with brown hair and dark brown eyes. Those dark brown eyes attracted me from the start; when she smiled they sparkled and dimples appeared in her cheeks. I well remember that flash of eyes and first friendly smile and the disturbing effect it had upon me. As I soon discovered, she smiled a lot; a laughing kind of smile that spread all over her rounded face and lingered round her generous mouth. Usually she wore those corduroy breeches and thick wool stockings, and it wasn't until some time later when she wore a frock that I noticed her shapely legs. A cheerful, good-natured, practical girl, with a strong sense of humour, Molly had all the charms and attributes I could possibly desire. With a little encouragement from Mr Clutterbuck—I was very shy in those days—it was only a matter of a few months before I was walking out with her.

At first we were very conscious that our neighbours would see us and as we walked together along our country lanes we kept a foot apart; then, as the weeks went by, we grew bolder and walked hand in hand, arm in arm. By that time we neither knew nor cared who saw us; we'd fallen in love with each other and nothing else seemed to matter very much.

The first time I took her to my home I remember the stiff atmosphere as we sat at the tea table; my father said little. When first introduced to Molly he'd said, 'How d'ye do' in a solemn voice, and later he'd remarked on the weather. But now, at table, he confined himself to comments such as 'another cup of tea please, Ethel'. I knew he was waiting for a moment when he could decently leave the table and bury himself in the *Daily Mail*.

My mother was being rather starchy and using a voice not quite her own. She was pouring tea, with one hand on the tea-pot lid; it was her treasured tea-set and rarely used. I knew she was frightened that a piece would get broken. And quite likely, too; there was just that air of tension when china falls from nervous fingers. However, Mother—while determined to create an impression—was at the same time scrutinising Molly; she kept giving her furtive, searching glances. Poor Molly, sitting very upright and her face a little pink, was enduring the ordeal remarkably well. But real conversation was impossible; I suppose I could have tried harder, but I was on edge, and when I did tentatively try Mother put on her disapproving look.

Fortunately, Uncle George, Father's elder brother arrived. Now Uncle George wasn't the man to be intimidated or to endure a stuffy silence. He walked into the room bringing a breath of fresh air—and a whiff of pigs.

'Give me a cup of tea, Ethel,' he said, with his customary gusto. 'I'm as dry as a bone. Me throat is parched and I've a touch of the wind.' He sat down and tugged at the grimy handkerchief knotted round his neck.

Mother cast him a spiteful look and her neck reddened. Silently she left the table to fetch him a cup and saucer.

'Hullo, our George,' said Father.

'Well, how be you all?' asked Uncle George, spreading himself at the table. 'How are you, Molly?' and turning to me with a wink, 'How's it goin' then?'

Mother returned with a second-best cup and saucer. 'You might', she said severely to Uncle George as she poured his tea, 'have cleaned yourself up and put on a clean collar and tie if you were coming to tea.'

'Now you do know how I hate collars and ties,' replied Uncle. 'Never did have much time for 'em. I'm a busy man an' it's blasted hot.'

'You knew we had a young lady coming to tea,' said Mother primly. But it was no good; the impression she'd hoped to create was in ruins, blown away by Uncle's rumbling laughter, frightened away by his good humoured, fat, ruddy, unshaven face. Even Father began to relax. He smiled, not much, but it was a start.

'Ah, young Molly here, her an' me's old friends,' said Uncle George. 'She's seen me many a time a lot rougher than I be now, when I've bin givin' Arthur Clutterbuck a hand.'

11

The corners of Mother's mouth drooped. She sighed and began to clear the table.

Six months later we were going down to Bristol by train, a Bristol still torn and ravaged by bombs, to meet Molly's parents. A firm handshake from her father and a sharp appraising look from stern eyes. I knew what he was thinking, 'Is this young man good enough for my daughter?' From her mother, a warm friendly smile and I felt immediately at ease with her—though I guessed she, too, was wondering, 'Is he suitable for my Molly? If I were her age would I choose a young man like him?'

It was a much happier session at their table. Molly's mother was very ready to talk and laugh. Her father asked me questions about farming, what prospect had farming now the war was over? And in a subtle way he was also enquiring into my prospects. Actually, my prospects were not very bright. I hoped with help from Uncle George, to rent a small farm; but farms to rent were hard to find. I put a gloss on my prospects, and he, kindly man, didn't press the point.

'See what her Mother's like', had been Jack Musgrove's advice, Jack worked with me at Suttridge Farm, 'cos that's how she'll be in thirty years time.' On that test Molly passed with flying colours; but then, she'd done that on her own account months ago.

Mrs Clutterbuck, of Willow Farm, was a placid woman, of rather frail appearance and with silver white hair. Her daughters were married with children of their own and both lived a considerable distance away; too far to be anything but infrequent visitors, and she had come to regard Molly almost as a daughter. They hadn't a son, a fact never spoken of but nevertheless a disappointment to them. Both Mr and Mrs Clutterbuck were getting old. Molly helped in the house, but it was a house too big for their needs, and a worry. With Molly's help there was no pressing cause for Mrs Clutterbuck to worry. But worry she did, as old people will when no longer active enough to cope with things themselves.

Some time ago Mr Clutterbuck had spoken vaguely of retirement, given the idea an airing as it were; then we heard no more about it. The farm was slipping back a bit, haymaking and harvesting became more protracted, and ploughing and planting got behind, but his reluctance to give up was understandable. No one is quite so much at a loss as the retired farmer, and to Mr Clutterbuck farming was more than just a way of life—it was all of life. He was a traditionalist; some said he was an old fool. He farmed more or less as his father and grandfather had farmed, making few concessions to modern methods. Stubborn perhaps. He still farmed with horses, refusing to have a tractor. His pedigree Shorthorn cows were still milked by hand. He kept his Shorthorn bullocks for beef, had a breeding flock of sheep, folded lambs on roots and still remained loyal to the native breed of pig, the Gloucester Old Spot. All food for his animals was produced on the farm; the four course rotation was still practised. There was much to commend his system, but unfortunately it was laborious, expensive, and now —with inadequate labour—slow and impractical. Two horses and a man slowly plodding up and down with a single furrow plough just couldn't compete with a tractor pulling two or three furrows and pulling them a great deal faster. Ernest Saggamore, the farmer at Suttridge had said, 'You get no more for wheat grown on horse ploughed land.' But bluff Arthur Clutterbuck didn't see it like that, he just puffed stolidly at his pipe and went on as before.

Even his beloved Shorthorns were becoming unfashionable. Before the war Shorthorns were seen on a vast majority of dairy farms; they were without doubt the dairy cow of England. But now they were in retreat, and the Friesian advanced. More and more of these distinctive black and white cattle could be seen as the years went by. First a few

13

among a herd of Shorthorns, then a few more. Farmers started using a Friesian bull on their Shorthorn cows, producing blue roan animals at the first cross, and soon more herds were completely black and white.

'Dual purpose', cried the Friesian men scornfully, 'no purpose.' Dual purpose, as the Shorthorns were, meant those capable of producing milk and beef; the heifers for milk and the bullocks for beef. It cannot be denied that unfortunately the heifers sometimes looked beefy and the bullocks had the dairy conformation. 'You must have dual purpose cows in England to produce calves for beef', argued Mr Clutterbuck, Mr Saggamore and others. And in time the Friesian did become dual purpose, thus copying the breed it had displaced.

Like me, Molly had become fond of Shorthorns. We would keep Shorthorns. 'If we have a farm', I said. 'When we have a farm', said Molly. Perhaps I was more aware of just how slender were our chances of finding a small farm to rent. But Molly was always hopeful; her cheerfulness and optimism were infectious. We strolled along our narrow lanes, hearts firmly entwined. We would marry, have a farm and raise a family of sons. The future was ours.

Our visits to the Crown incurred Mother's displeasure as she didn't approve of women going inside public houses. 'Oh, why don't you get him to go to church instead?' she asked Molly. Mother wasn't a regular church-goer herself, but she was keen for others to attend. Molly ignored her displeasure. 'It would be nice if they would both go to church on Sunday evenings', I overheard Mother say to her friend Mrs Peabody, the church organist. Although she never said in so many words, she left me in no doubt that she disapproved of Molly's wearing lipstick.

Molly liked dancing and we often went to the village

dances. I was a poor, reluctant dancer, and only the pangs of jealousy I suffered when I saw Molly dancing with somebody else made me shuffle round the floor. An evening at the cinema in town meant a rush to finish work in time to change and catch the train. As I hurried with the milking I prayed Mr Saggamore wouldn't find some job to delay me. Molly fared rather better as Mr Clutterbuck was more understanding about the needs of courtship. But it was often a frantic bicycle ride to the station, the porter holding up the train as we approached. We got accustomed to seeing the last half of the main film first and the beginning later. We became practised in a sprint through the streets to catch the last train home.

Jack Musgrove took an interest in our courtship, he obviously approved of Molly and was captivated by her ready smile. Nevertheless, he had advice to give—I'd never known a situation when he hadn't.

'They do say that choosing a wife is as difficult as choosing a hoss,' he said, 'but to my mind it's a sight more difficult; after all, you can always sell an unsatisfactory hoss. So you take care, see that she can cook and see that 'er do eat well. Them as don't eat much theirselves don't think as others need much grub. Grub is the makin' of marriage.'

I was able to reassure Jack on both these points. The open air life had given Molly a good appetite, and she often cooked at Willow Farm; I had opportunities to sample it. Mrs Clutterbuck had taught her to bake bread, to make many of our local dishes, to deal with the offal after pig killing and to kill, pluck and dress poultry. But even if Molly had not acquired these skills, it wouldn't have made the slightest difference.

'Ah,' said Jack, knowingly, 'there's more to marriage than looks. A full eye and a fair face will wither, and good legs will grow either fat or scrawny. But grub is grub. Grub's the makin' of marriage.'

15

'I've got a surprise for you, m'lads,' said Mr Saggamore as we sat milking in the cowshed one morning. 'You won't be sitting on these stools for much longer.' Jack Musgrove merely grunted and went on squirting milk into his bucket. Jack was in his late forties, married with one son, and had his own house and a couple of small orchards. He was a stockily built man, able to do any job on a farm, a good man to work with.

'What's that then, Boss?' asked Bill Lugg, a note of excitement in his voice. Bill, who usually muttered and grumbled quietly to himself as he worked, and walked with a slouching gait, would occasionally get excited for some trivial reason. These were the times when he would perform strange antics which Jack called 'doing didows'. These 'didows' were meant to impress, but like Bill's careless habits they invariably incurred the wrath of Saggamore.

However, Saggamore's anger never lasted long and Bill bore no resentment. "Im cussed and cussed I, aye 'im did, but 'im was all right atter, aye 'im was', Bill would say, a cheerful grin on his rough weather-beaten face.

Bill was younger than Jack; short and as strong as an ox, he seemed positively to enjoy hard, dull physical labour. 'I like summat I know I be at, aye I do', he'd say.

Bill wasn't married and lived with his mother, a fierce old woman with a sharp tongue and penetrating eyes. His younger brother Gritton who was also single lived with them. Bill thought very highly of Gritton. 'Our Grit, 'im says so, aye 'im do, an' our Grit do know, aye 'im do', we were frequently told.

Mr Saggamore's cryptic announcement had aroused Bill's interest, and getting no response Bill rose from his stool and bucket in hand, asked again, 'What's that then, Boss? What do you mean?'

'Sit down an' get on with your milkin',' replied Saggamore, 'I'll tell you when I'm ready and not afore.'

That was just like Ernest Saggamore. Unpredictable, a

man of uncertain moods, both kindly and harsh. Independent, heeding nobody's advice or opinions, completely his own master. Shrewd and energetic, farming with a sure instinct. He drove himself hard, asked no man to do anything that he wasn't prepared to do himself. Successful in bad times as well as good. Less successful farmers said that he was lucky, and so he was, even the weather seemed to co-operate with him. But I'd been at Suttridge long enough to know that mere luck was not the only factor involved in his success. Though I'd never been able to make up my mind if it was an angel he had on his shoulder or a devil at his heels.

'What's 'im mean? I'd aim as 'im's goin' to sell the cows, aye 'im is,' said Bill when Mr Saggamore had left us.

'Just as likely to buy 'alf a dozen more, if I know 'im,' said Jack. 'He's like the weather, you never know what he's goin' to do next.'

For once, I thought Bill might be right. Mr Saggamore didn't like cows very much, he was more of an arable, beef and sheep man. He begrudged the time spent with the cows, but the cows provided a regular income, and calves to grow into beef.

'If 'im's gwaine to get rid of the cows', muttered Bill, that afternoon, 'old Caleb wun't like it, aye 'im wun't.'

'Caleb ain't here now, so I don't see as that's much odds,' replied Jack. Caleb Pocock was a small thick-set elderly man, bow-legged, and with tiny, bright eyes peering out of a fresh complexioned face so lined with broken veins that it resembled a road map. He was cantankerous, artful and parsimonious and disapproved of all modern farming methods and machinery—contemptuously referring to all machines as 'contraptions'. He could, when it suited his purpose, flatter, cajole and wheedle—and if these did not serve he would produce a flow of tears. He frequently spoke of God and heaven and the wonder of his conversion—all in the most unctuous terms and very embarrassing to those of us who had to listen to him.

'Aargh,' I'd heard Caleb say, when somebody had upset him, 'I've more money than that bugger'll ever have. I'll show him one day.'

Despite the fact that farmworkers were poorly paid, old Caleb, by stinting and saving, by selling vegetables grown in his garden, by keeping a few pigs and doing several little extra jobs in his spare time, had managed to collect together a nice little sum of money—as he never tired of telling us. I'd often seen him sitting in the cowshed, counting a thick wad of banknotes.

He'd recently retired, but we still saw him; leaning over his garden gate, still wearing breeches, leggings and heavy hobnailed boots, waiting to waylay someone to whom he could talk about the iniquities of modern farming, and of his impending death. 'The good Lord will soon be sending for me,' he'd say. But as he stood there, clutching his garden gate with loose fleshed hands, he seemed to be clinging tenaciously to life.

'I've ordered a milking machine,' Mr Saggamore said a few days later. 'One of us 'ull be able to cope with the milking then. I've got tired of all of us squatting in here twice a day when we could be out in the fields.'

Most dairy farmers now had milking machines, but only a month or so ago Mr Saggamore had been roundly declaring that he wouldn't have one on the place. Perhaps the departure of Caleb had helped to make him change his mind. The general shortage of labour was one of the principal reasons why farmers were turning more and more to machinery. The war, the urgent need to grow more food, the ploughing-up campaign, the coming of the tractor and the War Agricultural Committee had brought great changes. And change breeds change.

18

Then, there'd been the German and Italian prisoners of war to help at peak periods as well as the Irishmen and the land girls at the hostel. But now they'd all gone, the only land girls left were the ones with regular employment on farms.

Because of the difficulty in getting suitable workers, and because farmers at last had some money, there was an increasing demand for machines. Although machines like everything else were in short supply, there's nothing like scarcity to stimulate demand. It was a time of austerity, but it was also a time of hope. Old men like Caleb might decry new ways, and the countryman's talk was liberally spiced with affectionate reminiscences, but most people thought tomorrow would be a better day. Change and progress were still thought to be synonymous.

In the autumn a young ex-R.A.F. pilot, Ben, came to instal the machine and the petrol engine to drive it, and to instruct us—and the cows—in its use. An ebullient young man, with blonde hair and a large handle-bar moustache. His conversation was peppered with expressions such as 'bang-on', 'wizard prang', and 'good (or bad) show'. When the machine, vacuum pump, pipes and taps in the stalls and the petrol engine were installed, Ben, brimming over with friendliness and gusto, set about teaching us how to milk the cows, and the cows how to be milked.

The cows did not take kindly to the idea, the more timid the cow the more violently she reacted. 'Oh, poor show!' exclaimed Ben as a machine bucket and cluster were sent hurtling into the gutter. He grinned cheerfully as he rubbed his leg after being kicked by a startled cow. Lids rolled off upturned buckets, and milk ran over the cowshed floor. 'Early days yet', he said to Mr Saggamore, who, to judge by his expression, was already regretting having bought the machine.

'I don't know,' said Mr Saggamore sourly surveying the pandemonium which was now a twice daily occurence in the cowshed, 'other people seem to like 'em, but I'm damned if I do.'

The cows were frightened by the strange buckets and tubes, by the ticking of the pulsators and the pop, pop, pop, of the engine. And, of course, we were clumsy with the machine; we found it difficult, despite all Ben's careful advice and instructions, to fix the machine to the cows' teats. Like a lot of things it's easy enough when you know how, but we held the clusters of teat cups awkwardly and let air hiss. The cows objected to this hissing, quite understandably; no doubt to them the hissing had a sinister sound. Up went their feet, bang, clatter went a bucket, louder hisses from the stall tap as the connecting tube was wrenched away, startling all the other cows, making them shuffle about, pull back on their ties, lift their tails and dung, which shot everywhere—they were still out at grass and their dung was sloppy. Some cows didn't bother to lift their tails, but after dunging flicked their dirty tails and slapped us in the face as we struggled to milk them.

'They say', said Mr Saggamore, after consulting a friend who praised machines, 'that heyfers will come in and take to it like one o'clock. It's only old cows used to hand milking what do play old Harry. But, by gum, it takes some believing. I was a fool to be talked into it, damned if I weren't.'

One afternoon in the midst of this commotion, old Caleb came hobbling into the shed; his face was black with rage. He studied the scene taking every little detail of it in, saying nothing at first, just moving his lips. At last he could contain himself no longer.

'God Almighty!' he said. 'What in heaven's name have come over you Boss?' he demanded.

Mr Saggamore remained silent. Later he told us he wouldn't have had Caleb arrive then. No, not for a thousand pounds, he wouldn't.

'It ain't any good,' said Caleb grimly, 'I can't understand what have come over you, allowing such a thing.'

Saggamore looked ill at ease, but said nothing. After all, he must have been wondering the same thing.

'If you don't get rid of that contraption, it'll ruin you and the cows. It'll give 'em all bad quarters, it'll dry 'em all off. It'll make their milk as poor as water, cows can't give good milk when they be scarified like that. It'll make 'em slip their calves.'

Caleb gave the machine one last savage look before stumping off, muttering, 'You must be off yer 'ead. God forgive me.'

'They'll get used to it soon,' said Ben, 'and so will you.'

And so it proved. The machine lightened and speeded up the labour of milking. But neither Mr Saggamore nor Jack really liked the machine. On Ben's last day, I overheard them discussing it. Heads close together, Mr Saggamore gesticulating slightly, using his large hands as adjunct to speech; Jack solemn, nodding his head and standing with his legs apart.

'There's only one place for that machine, Jack,' said Mr Saggamore, quietly and seriously, in a confiding, almost conspiratorial manner.

As he spoke, Jack regarded him dolefully, with his head slightly cocked to catch every word—Jack was getting a bit deaf.

'Yes,' pronounced Mr Saggamore, 'there's only one place for that machine, Jack,' and he pointed to the dungheap outside the cowshed. Jack nodded his head in agreement.

Bill flatly refused to have anything to do with the machine, he had never liked cows and I suspect he saw a good opportunity to escape their tyranny. One must, I feel, like cows to be able to endure the constraints imposed by twice daily milking, midnight calvings and so on.

So I became cowman, tying myself, as they say, to the cow's tail; and with a knot so firm it has remained until the present day.

21

CHAPTER TWO

News from the Village

The village in which I lived with my parents was some two miles from Suttridge Farm. Besides having a church, chapel, school, police station, and post office, the village had two grocery shops—one of which sold clothes—a butcher, baker, boot shop, newsagent, and three public houses.

My father had a shop; a homely jumble of hardware, farm and garden sundries. Pitch forks, manure forks, spades, shovels, wooden hay rakes, hoes, axes and hedge bills stood around the walls, like a motley army off duty. Rolls of barbed wire and wire netting in the corners; pots, pans, lanterns, bill hooks, balls of string, rat and mole traps and rabbit snares were suspended from the ceiling. Oil lamps stood on shelves. Scythes dangled from hooks on the walls; locks, knives, screws and nails were kept in boxes behind the counter, and so were the smaller tools. Milking utensils, buckets, brushes and brooms seemed to jostle with each other for what space there was, and often succeeded in tripping up an unwary customer. The smells of paraffin, creosote, of blood and bone, hoof and horn fertiliser permeated the whole shop.

Some things sold better than others, some didn't seem to sell at all. Of the latter, Father would remark, 'not much call for 'em.' But it didn't worry him for he believed in keeping a comprehensive stock. Some day, somebody might 'call for 'em' and he would be able to supply. 'And that', said Father, 'is what I'm here for.' More of a worry was the difficulty in obtaining stock as many things were still in short supply.

There was a loss of trade to the town but, despite the gloomy prognostications, the village shopkeepers were still holding on, and most of the day to day essentials could be bought in the village. Few people had motor cars, petrol was rationed anyway. There was a good train service to the market town and yet many people, even the young, did not leave the village for weeks on end. Some farmers now had motor cars and drove to market each week, often their wives accompanying them to do the shopping. Some village women went fortnightly or monthly to town by train. But the majority of older country people, certainly the men, still spoke of the market town as a distant place and rarely paid a visit there.

Mrs Hatch, the newsagent, was one person who constantly struck a discordant note in the harmony of the community. Before the war she'd been tiresome, she 'allowed' her customers to have newspapers provided they behaved themselves, which meant they meekly endured her tantrums and abuse. During the war she became downright awkward, as well as conducting vicious campaigns against the farmers. Shortly after the war had started she'd become a regular church-goer, but her behaviour—contrary to the sanguine hopes of some—had rapidly deteriorated. We rarely saw her husband, Ebenezer, who spent his time mysteriously at the back of the shop. Nobody ever discovered what he did, but he must have been busy. Mrs Hatch wasn't the sort of woman to leave anyone in peace and certainly she would not have allowed her husband to sit around idle. It couldn't have been pleasant living with Mrs Hatch. Perhaps even slow-witted Ebenezer had realised this at last; twelve months ago he departed from life.

After Ebenezer's death, Mrs Hatch quarrelled with Mr Bence, the vicar. Poor old Mr Bence had no idea what it was all about and neither did anyone else, but she abused him publicly and at every available opportunity. She had, she told everyone, reported him to the bishop. Dr Higgins suffered even worse; she accused him of murdering her husband and she had reported him, or so she said, to the Home Secretary, the Chief Constable, the Medical Council, the Medical Officer of Health, and to her M.P. She was vindictive, telling everyone who would listen—and most had to listen if they still wanted a newspaper—the most malicious stories about the doctor. You may wonder why she wasn't sued for slander. But people like Mrs Hatch, while constantly threatening to sue others are rarely sued themselves.

Alfred Tucker, the butcher, must also be mentioned here, if only because he was at this time constantly mentioning himself and his plans. Alfred had recently bought six acres of land and proposed to go in for pig breeding in a very big way.

'I shall have a look round first,' Alfred told us in The Crown one evening. 'I want nothing but the best, the very best.' Here Alfred paused; then after shifting his stance a little so that his legs were further astride, he continued, 'The best, the very best is only just good enough for Alfred Tucker. I need good foundation stock, it'll take some finding, but I'll find it. None of this old fashioned nonsense, all the latest methods, that's my style. I'll bide my time, it'll probably mean a trip to Denmark, but when I start', Alfred looked rather fierce now, and raised his voice, 'I'll show everyone a thing or two, as you'd expect from Alfred Tucker. Yes, yes,' now Alfred lowered his voice and his little eyes gleamed, 'I shall go into pig breeding in a big way, a very big way.'

'Everything up to the minute, eh?' asked mild Mr Teakle of the boot shop, quietly.

'That's about the size of it,' said Alfred, with evident satisfaction.

'Big,' said Uncle George later, 'Alfred Tucker allus was big. You'd expect Alfred to talk and do things in a big way. Big talk from a big man, Alfred allus was a big talker. That bit of ground have gone to his head, but there, whisky costs money, talk costs nothing.' Uncle George spoke slowly, bringing a sneer into every syllable. He was nettled that Alfred Tucker had not sought his advice as he regarded himself as an authority on pigs.

In fact Uncle George regarded himself as an authority on many things. On fruit and vegetable growing, cider and wine making, on doctors and patent medicines, murder and scandal, to mention only a few. Uncle had a smallholding just outside the village. He was rotund and redfaced, getting old and a bit short of breath. Nevertheless, he could still play a merry trick or two, still inject life with a touch of magic, still get himself into scrapes and contradict himself with alacrity. He couldn't be kept down, in fact he often said, 'You can't keep a good man down.' And nobody was left in any doubt that Uncle George, in Uncle George's opinion, was a good man. He was an incurable gossip, and if rumour lacked scandal he invariably inserted it. When accused of making mischief, Uncle was quite unabashed. 'Mischief-making?' he said, 'I d'love it.'

Only those who have lived without electricity can realise the difference it made. When it was first installed in the village by the Electricity Board it meant light more than anything else. No more oil lamps with their attendant duties of cleaning, filling and lighting. No more going to bed by candlelight, the guttering candle dropping hot wax. Less trade, incidentally, for my father. To say that it was a boon is to state the obvious; not so obvious perhaps was that it was another step towards the villager's reliance on the townsman. A few of the older villagers were not enthusiastic, they didn't think they'd bother with it. A great many said they wouldn't like their food cooked by electricity, it wouldn't taste the same. For the first few years electricity was used almost exclusively for lighting; I don't suppose many more than two dozen power points were fixed. But my mother wanted an electric cooker, vacuum cleaner, immersion heater, kettle, iron and I don't know what else besides.

'Steady on, old lady,' said Father, 'let's go careful over this here 'lectric. It's going to cost money.'

'That's right, think of your pocket, never mind me,' replied Mother, her hopes dashed and her temper rising. 'You never consider me, working my fingers to the bone, cleaning lamps, hawking buckets of coal, stoking fires, cleaning grates, and down on my hands and knees brushing and scrubbing. Dorothea's got everything and I can have nothing. I made a mistake marrying into this family, as mean as dirt the lot of you.' Dorothea was Mother's sister. Her husband was a bank manager and they lived in London.

'Dorothea's husband will soon be retiring and have a pension from the bank, and what will we have? Nothing, not a penny,' said Mother, her temper giving way to self-pity. She shot a glance at me. 'And what about him? I never wanted him to go to work on a farm. I warned you. But you and that great lump of a George persuaded me. And what will become of him? Eh? Answer me that. He'll end his days as a farm labourer and retire without a pension. That George said he'd help him to become a farmer, and what's he done about it? Nothing. No farm, nothing. I could sit down and howl.'

'Our George ain't none too keen on this 'lectric,' said Father, just as if he hadn't heard a word of Mother's tirade.

'Oh, that cratur! He's at the back of it is he? I might have guessed it,' cried Mother.

'Our George have got a head on him like a lawyer.'

'More like a turnip and about as much sense,' snapped Mother as she left the room.

Later I heard Mother muttering to herself, 'Another bad egg. I thought I'd have some nice electric things like Dorothea, but it's turned out another bad egg. Oh and I did so want an electric boiler, but I get nothin'. Nobody ever thinks of me.'

Uncle George decided not to have electricity; he thought the light would be too harsh, it would hurt his eyes. He preferred the soft glow of an oil lamp. Then he changed his mind and had it installed, just one light in the kitchen and with the lowest powered bulb obtainable. That was the full extent of his installation, but even so he kept muttering, 'God knows what it'll cost, daresay it'll run away with a mint o' money during the course of a twelve-month.' And at a later date, 'That 'lectric ain't all it's cracked up to be. That 'lectric light's no company, not like me old oil lamp. I'd go back to me old lamp if I hadn't parted with all that money havin' the 'lectric put in.'

Some years later the District Council piped a supply of water to the village. Previously water was pumped or drawn from a well; some households had to carry water from a pump in the street. In a dry summer water became scarce, then jealousy, acrimony and feuds ensued. Women accused each other of having more than their share and of wasting water. With mains water there was plenty for everyone; clean water too, and free of insects, slugs, and other unidentified bodies. An endless supply, just by turning a tap. Mains water was at first a blessing but it was very soon taken as a matter of course.

When building restrictions were lifted—I go forward in time—bathrooms and flush lavatories were installed, cess pits dug. Ironically, when there was an abundant supply of water and better hygiene facilities, the village began to stink. Previously, when water had to be used sparingly, our primitive drainage was adequate, but now it couldn't cope with all the additional water being used.

An even more fundamental change came to village life. Before the war nearly all the men worked in or around the surrounding countryside, and then, attracted by higher wages, they went to work in factories some miles distant. Their work had no connection with the countryside, the village only a place to return to after work. Young men grew up not knowing a hay fork from a dung fork; yet at one time most village lads could harness a horse and lead a loaded wagon through a narrow gateway. Then they looked to the town for their money, food and pleasure. The countryside just became a series of fields with grass and corn in them—it's doubtful if they knew which was which—and the village became just a dormitory.

Many years later, the process went even further for as men left the land, cottages became vacant. Many of these cottages were in poor condition and despised by the local people. The young wanted modern houses. Then the townsmen saw these cottages, possibly through rose-coloured spectacles, fell in love with them and bought them. They obtained grants and did them up, though the 'improvements', such as large windows, often destroyed the character of the houses. But perhaps they were by order of local councils, or maybe I am prejudiced. The real countryman doesn't like large windows; when he's indoors he likes to feel shut in, so much of his working life is spent in the open air. Whereas the townsman, condemned to spending his working life indoors, wants just the reverse.

Once local people saw what could be done with these old cottages they began to resent townspeople occupying them, especially when they were used as weekend cottages. They began to want back what they'd so recently despised, but demand from the townspeople pushed prices beyond their reach.

However, these developments took place long after the period covered in this book. I must return to the time when no vacant house or cottage could be found. And this was our problem, Molly's and mine, for we hoped to marry. But no house, let alone a farm, could be found.

Molly was optimistic; she was sure something would turn up, but I had doubts and I knew she received letters from Bristol urging her to return. I couldn't really have blamed her if she had, but she remained at Willow Farm. And when we met we made plans for the future; we dreamed dreams and talked the fond, foolish talk of young lovers.

CHAPTER THREE

Changing Ways

Change in the countryside has been a continuing process. But never before now had there been such a swift change, such sudden application of new methods by so many.

Shortage of labour was a factor, but the ploughing-up campaign during the last war had been the real turning point. That was when the tractor had come into its own: tractors unlike horses did not tire and the rule of the horse was broken. However, until the advent of the versatile Ferguson tractor with its hydraulically attached and controlled implements, the tractor had only been a mechanical substitute for the draught horse. The Ferguson System revolutionised agriculture.

But the horse had bred its own replacement and its food had been grown on the farm. New tractors had to be bought and so did the fuel to drive them. This meant that farms became less self-sufficient. The dung heap was neglected, rotation of crops was ignored, fertility could be purchased by the bag, science would provide magical short cuts; or so it was claimed. By and by, farmers became processors rather than husbandmen.

The 1947 Agricultural Act had a profound effect. It gave farming guaranteed markets and prices, and various grants and subsidies—which brought cries of 'feather-bedded farmers.' Some people thought it was a bit immoral food producers making a profit by their skill, labour and production. But, as one Wiltshire farmer and writer pointed out, these guaranteed prices and markets were given at a time when there was a shortage of food and when world prices were higher than those fixed for the British farmer.

The Act brought more interference from the politicians and bureauocrats, from economists and other pundits. It brought the annual February price review and exhortations for increased efficiency, more regulations and forms to be filled. The National Agricultural Advisory Service, commonly called the NAAS, came into being with its bright young men intent on teaching farmers how to farm. To these young men all farming problems could be solved on paper. They could and did show that farming was a profitable occupation, again on paper. The War Agricultural Executive Committee that had wielded such power during the war years, became the County Agricultural Executive Committee. But farmers still called it the War Ag and it retained its powers of dispossession.

However, the stability that the Act gave to farming must have been welcome. A farmer could now plan ahead with confidence and be sure of selling his produce for a reasonable price. There was no longer the need to spend hours

31

'watching the markets', or haggling over the price of a fat beast or a ton of corn with butchers, merchants and dealers. The farmer could devote all his energy to producing food. Some of the older farmers were a bit wary, fearing the Act would be abolished once the food emergency was over, and when it suited the politicians. Cheap food being a traditional vote-catcher, as it was, there were many who said the government was 'throwing money at farmers'. In vain did the farmer try to explain that the subsidies went to the consumer not the producer.

Perversely perhaps, many of the older farmers missed those hours and hours of haggling. Some of them, Mr Saggamore included, had enjoyed the haggling, it was almost the breath of life to them.

The guaranteed prices related only to the finished product; with store animals and breeding stock farmers could still indulge in the uncertainty of the auction or the haggling of a private deal. Mr Saggamore much preferred the private transaction and he was a past master at it. Sometimes I accompanied him on spring, summer, or autumn evenings when he went to a farm to buy store cattle. Stores are animals that are still growing but have not yet reached the final stage of fattening.

To observe Mr Saggamore buying cattle was to see a master at his trade. He would inspect the cattle carefully, walking round to view them from all angles, taking particular notice of their 'rear end', perhaps pulling his hat down on his brow and narrowing his eyes. Making no comment, just looking at them. Another long last look at them from the gateway, but still no comment. Then he, and the man who was selling, would walk back to the house or go to look at some crop on the farm. Every few yards they would stop, face each other, and talk about everything but the cattle they'd just seen.

Once inside the house they would settle down to a glass of

whisky and talk again. They reminisced of old times, or speculated on the future. They talked of everything except the cattle Mr Saggamore had come to see. At last he would rise to go. His host would prevail on him to have one more drink—which he would have—then a long farewell at the door. Mr Saggamore would turn and make for his car, his host following.

About ten or twenty yards from the house, the car would halt; one of them had remembered an amusing incident from the past. Windows down and car door open, they would start chatting again. They hadn't forgotten the store cattle, but neither cared to mention them until the last possible moment; one not wishing to appear over eager to sell, the other not wishing to seem too keen to buy.

'Oh, and about that little bunch of cattle,' Mr Saggamore would casually remark at last. 'Ah', would be the other's reply, 'did you like the look of 'em?'

'Nice little cattle.' Mr Saggamore would never run anything down which he wanted to buy, unlike some dealers. It was assumed that they were good cattle if he showed any interest in them.

'Ah, they'd do well with you.'

'I daresay, at the right price.' This would be said very slowly.

'You know me. When have you found me unreasonable?' Not really a question, but a statement, this.

'Well, what do you want for 'em?' Mr Saggamore is sharp; his slow, casual disinterested manner gone.

Now the real business would begin. A figure would be mentioned. Mr Saggamore would appear shocked, throw his hands up in a mock horror and exclaim: 'Begod! D'ya want to ruin me?' He would state a much lower figure and now it would be the other's turn to look shocked and take a few paces back, as if recoiling in disgust. 'Be reasonable, Ernest.'

'Come on now. What'll you take?'

The seller would suggest a slightly lower price than he'd first mentioned. Saggamore would then make a marginally better offer. And so it would go on, each taking turn to appear shocked, indignant, angry; patient but tired with such nonsensical high or low prices. The gap would close gradually to cries from both of 'I'm trying to meet you', cries of exasperation. Eventually, there wouldn't be much difference, but still they wouldn't be able to agree, indeed at this stage both became vehement. Once again Mr Saggamore would start the car, shout another figure, and when the other shook his head start to drive away, then stop, and thrusting his head through the window make another offer. Or the seller would poke his head into the car with another price. 'Done!' one or the other would say, and an outstretched hand would be slapped. At last the deal was clinched.

Last year we'd used a sweep for much of our haymaking at Suttridge. Fixed to the front of the tractor, its long wooden prongs gathered the hay from the windrow and pushed it to the stack in the field. We pitched the hay into an elevator which dropped it on top of the stack. This system did away with the loading and unloading of wagons, and no time was wasted travelling back and forth. 'By gum,' Mr Saggamore had exclaimed, 'this is a topping job. You can get some hay together like this.'

We all thought it a topping job. Jack liked it because he could stay on the rick. 'It don't half save my poor old fit,' he said. Bill working beside Jack also approved, 'I know what I be at, aye I do,' he muttered. And I, pitching the hay into the elevator, soon fell into a steady rhythm. Mr Saggamore drove the tractor, his tie flowing over his shoulder—nothing would induce him to remove his collar and tie. Nothing, for that matter, would induce Jack to remove his waistcoat.

'By gum, we can get over some ground,' Mr Saggamore would shout above the noise of the tractor and elevator.

Caleb hobbled out to view the spectacle.

'I don't hold with that contraption,' he observed, 'it'll rip up green grass and set the rick afire.'

During our second year of using the sweep, Mr Saggamore told us that he wouldn't be using the wagons and hayloader this year when we came to put hay in the barn. 'I've got a chap coming with his baler and tractor,' he said. 'We'll sweep the hay to the baler and haul the bales into the barn, it'll be a quicker job.'

'Rugman's got Tommy Henwood and his pick-up baler,' said Jack. 'It's a nobby way of haymaking. Tommy just drives the baler along the wally and out pops parcels of hay. Rugman and his man just go and pick 'em up.'

But Mr Saggamore didn't like the idea. 'It'll make mushroomy hay, Jack. When he comes to use that hay, it'll smell like mushrooms.'

So we swept hay and forked it into the stationery baler. Two men were kept busy threading and tying the wire that bound the hay. The bales were big and heavy.

'That pick-up baler makes handy little bales,' Jack said. 'And Rugman and his men can pop out in the evening and clear a field.'

'There might be summat to be said for those pick-up balers,' Mr Saggamore said, weakening a little.

A few days later Jack had a further report. 'Them bales that Rugman stacked in his barn have all fallen down. Terrible mess, all over the place and half of 'em be bust.'

'I knew there'd be a snag to it. Them little bales tied up with string as the baler's goin' along won't stack. Not like these nice solid bales done up with wire,' Mr Saggamore said.

'Those bales of our'n be some heavy buggers. 'Nough to bust our chitt'lin's,' replied Jack.

'Got to kip up with the times, Jack. I ain't goin' back to that loadin' and unloadin' loose hay, it do take too long. I've a mind to have one of them pick-up's next year. I shall have one of my own mind. I don't fancy havin' to rely on a contractor. While you was waitin' for them your hay could spoil.'

However, he did have a contractor to combine some of his corn that year. Most of it was cut with the binder, stooked, loaded on wagons and stacked, but the last field of wheat was combined.

The combine and its work were startling, obliterating a scene that had stretched back for centuries, of many toilers in the harvest field. Doing away with the age old ritual of stooking, the pitching of sheaves, the loading and unloading of wagons, of stacking and thatching and threshing. One day a field of standing golden ripe corn, the next a field of bare stubble.

Just after Christmas Mr Saggamore ordered a pick-up baler from Mr Troy. 'Troy says everybody's doin' the same,' said Saggamore 'but there's not many of 'em about. He says he'll see me all right, though. Troy's a good sort.'

By Easter there was still no news of the baler; it wasn't needed yet, but Saggamore got impatient. Just before setting off for market, he'd say, 'I'll see what Troy's playing at, it's time that baler was here. I'll have to speak sharply to him today.' On returning Mr Saggamore would appear calmer, although he had no news of the baler. 'Troy says he'll see that I get one. Troy's a good chap.'

But the weeks went by and still no baler. Saggamore would mutter threats before market and express doubt on return. 'I can't understand Troy, he's very cagey. I hope he ain't goin' to let us down. I've dealt with him for years and allus paid on the nail—which is more than many can say. I'll give him a bit longer and then, by Harry, if a baler ain't standin' here, I'll let rip.'

The baler arrived just as we were about to mow the first field. 'We'll be all right now, lads,' said Mr Saggamore. 'Now we've got that baler. I'm glad I never got rasty with Troy. He's a good sort, I knew he'd see me all right.'

Caleb, who might have scorned the 'contraption' was unable to walk out to the hayfield. Crippled with arthritis, it was as much as he could do to hobble with the aid of two sticks to his garden gate. He'd sold the last of his pigs, the sties at the bottom of his garden were empty, his garden was becoming neglected. His housekeeper was elderly, too, and it was as much as she could do to cope with Caleb, let alone the garden. Caleb himself was a pitiful sight; his face had shrunk and his cunning little eyes had receded and lost their brightness. We could see that he had more than arthritis wrong with him. 'I'm gwain to die,' he said, in a torpid voice. It was difficult to know what to say to the old chap as you looked at him and saw that his words were true. 'I be agwain to die,' he would repeat, and little tears rolled down his cheeks. They were real tears now.

Poor old Caleb would have had much to criticise about our first year of pick-up baling. Most of the hay was mediocre stuff—it took farmers a few years to master the technique of making good hay with the baler. The bales tumbled out of the stack; Mr Saggamore swore and said 'must 'ave been clean off m'head to ever buy the bloody baler.' The knotters went wrong and failed to tie both strings, leaving a trail of broken bales across the field. Saggamore roared, 'Why can't we get on like other people? When I see Troy, I'll tell him he's sold me a damned bad bugger.'

Not only did we find the bales difficult to stack— 'squampy', Mr. Saggamore called them—but also awkward to handle, there was no rhythm to it, unlike previous methods of haymaking. 'I don't like carryin' parcels of hay,' said Jack, 'it ain't natural.'

'You've only got to look at the buggers and they fall to pieces or fall down,' said Bill 'aye 'em do. And you've only to turn your back and they do fall down, aye 'em do. They be sods, aye 'em be. Giv' I the old way where I know what I be at, that's what I say, aye, I do.'

'Rugman do swear by it,' said Jack, it being Rugman's second season with bales.

'And I do swear at it,' retorted Saggamore, who was busily engaged in tying the corner bales of the stack with twine in an attempt to stop them from slipping. 'There', he said when he finished an intricate system of twine and knots, 'I hope that'll stop the buggers from spewing out.'

A Saturday afternoon in late October. I was pulling mangolds. No sugar beet was grown now or potatoes, but we still grew turnips and swedes for sheep-folding and a few acres of mangolds for the cattle. I was alone. Jack and Bill had finished at mid-day and I was working in the mangold field until milking time. It was a warm afternoon and I worked with my jacket off and my sleeves rolled up. The mellow sun gave the afternoon a richness, enhancing the gold, the yellow and the red of the mangolds, and the leaves of the hedgerows and trees which were just beginning to turn. The earth was dry and crumbly, and as I cut off the leaves and flung the mangolds on to a heap the earth that had been clinging to the hairy roots fell off. I was reminded of my first experience of mangold pulling at Suttridge. Would this be my last?

Should I leave Suttridge? There seemed little future for me there. But what else should I do? What else *could* I do? Farming was the only trade I knew. Put like that my prospects weren't good. A house? A little farm? The chances seemed as remote as ever. And there was Molly, those letters from her parents. Perhaps she'd suddenly decide to return to

Bristol. Perhaps tonight, that's what she'd say. Return and meet a young man with a steady job, a pension on retirement; may be a bank clerk—my mother's words recurred to me—and live in a neat little suburban semi-detached house. No. Molly would never do that. And yet if Mr Clutterbuck did retire she wouldn't stop at Willow Farm.

Mr Saggamore came into the field, removed his jacket and worked beside me. Most of the time we worked in silence, but occasionally he made remarks like 'Father always loved mangold pulling' or 'devil of a good crop of mangolds.'

The sun was going down, sinking behind the hill, its last beams lingering on the field. The sun was red and its rosy light gave the heaps of mangolds a rich, ripe splendour. Mr Saggamore stopped working and straightened his back. He pulled a watch from his waistcoat pocket and said, 'It's gettin' on for milkin' time. We'll cover the heaps up.'

We walked to the end of the field and got two forks. As we flung the mangold leaves over the first heaps he said, 'There's goin' to be a sharpish frost to-night, I'll warrant.'

Again we worked in silence. Mr Saggamore seemed preoccupied. Once or twice I thought he was going to speak but then he seemed to change his mind. We were covering the last heap, half of it remained to be done. Mr Saggamore stopped working. He stuck his fork in the ground and leaned on it. I paused, he looked at me, straight in the eye, his broad-brimmed hat pulled low over his brow. The sun had almost disappeared behind the hill, there was a chill in the air.

'Clutterbuck's givin' up next Michaelmas,' he said. A long pause and then, 'I'm lettin' Barnard have his place.' Another pause. 'That'll leave Barnard's little place vacant.'

Mr Saggamore caught hold of his fork and began throwing the remaining leaves over the heap of mangolds. Then hesitantly, almost shyly, he said, 'That little place just over yonder would suit you.'

39

CHAPTER FOUR

From this day forward

The following summer, between haymaking and harvest, Molly and I were married. I had tentatively suggested a register office, but we were married at our parish church.

Molly's two younger sisters, Pamela and Sarah, who were to be the bridesmaids, came with Molly's mother a week before the wedding day and stayed with the Clutterbucks and Molly at Willow Farm. The farmhouse became the centre of much activity. Molly's mother was busily finishing the dresses for bride and bridesmaids. There were discussions about flowers, guests, seating arrangements, and other preparations. And like many a bridegroom I soon discovered that, though a necessary part of the ceremony,

I was an unfortunate encumbrance to the proceedings.

Three of Molly's maiden aunts came and stayed at The Crown. Two were sisters of Molly's father, the third was the eldest sister of her mother. Her father's sisters were gaunt and angular, her mother's sister was a buxom woman. All of them were in a state of suppressed excitement, and all of them insisted on kissing me repeatedly. Uncle George, who couldn't resist poking his nose into everything, observed their gushing behaviour and remarked to me, 'They women seem to have taken a fancy to you.'

The rest of Molly's relatives, her elder sister and husband, grandparents, aunts, uncles, cousins, second cousins and friends, were coming by train on the morning of the wedding.

On the evening before our wedding Willow Farm became a place of chatter and laughter. The activity, or apparent activity, became intense. Much of this was due to the presence of Molly's three maiden aunts. They talked incessantly and giggled—Mr Clutterbuck had been plying them with sherry. They worried about tomorrow's arrangements. They repeatedly asked Molly's mother and Mrs Clutterbuck if they were absolutely sure about the flowers in the church. They wondered if the bride's and bridesmaids' bouquets would arrive in time. They had, they all declared, known times when the bouquets had not arrived. They couldn't sit still but had to dart about, seeing to this and that, rushing off to see the wedding dress yet again. They teased each other about Uncle George, fluttered their hands, made a great fuss of Molly and declared they wouldn't sleep a wink that night. Molly's mother and sisters were less excitable. But Molly was the most composed female in the house, even the normally tranquil Mrs Clutterbuck was infected by it all. Not one of them had the slightest time for Mr Clutterbuck or me. 'Let's step outside,' suggested Mr Clutterbuck, 'this is no place for men.' We stood in the quiet, cool courtyard, the air redolent with the sweet smell of jasmine. Mr Clutterbuck studied the sky and said, 'It'll be a fine day tomorrow.'

Next morning I shaved with extra care. My father had warned, 'Times like this when you nick yourself and when the bleeding won't stop.' I fumbled with buttons, studs and cuff-links. My mother was in a fluster, continually patting her hair which she'd had permed the day before. 'Are your shoes clean?' she asked. 'Is your tie straight?' Admonishing my father—furtively looking at the *Daily Mail*—'Oh, do leave that paper alone today of all days. Do go and get yourself ready.' And to her sister Dorothea, who had come from London two days earlier, 'Do I look all right?' 'Shall I wear the other hat after all?' And to herself, 'I do hope that George will behave himself.' My father roused himself and went to get ready.

Aunt Dorothea remarked in her prim, precise way, 'Egbert has a morning suit. Of course, he couldn't leave the bank.'

'I quite understand,' replied Mother. 'Oh dear, I do hope it goes off all right.'

'She seems a nice girl,' I heard Aunt Dorothea say as I left the house with Tom, my best man. Tom was a friend from my schooldays and himself recently married.

The iron churchyard gates, the only ornamental gates in the parish to have escaped the salvage drive during the war, were usually kept closed. And when pushed open they groaned on their protesting rusty hinges. But this morning they were open and Tom and I walked nimbly through the gateway and up the flagged path to the church. Once inside the churchyard we walked more sedately, butterflies fluttered around the tombstones on either side of us. The tombstones were weathered by age and covered by moss and lichen; they reclined in various directions like tired old men in repose.

'Have you got the ring?'

Tom felt in his waistcoat pocket and assured me he had the ring. Over on the hill a farmer was still gathering hay.

'We finished last week, good thing too with this job coming off today,' said Tom. 'Has Clutterbuck finished?'

'Five days ago; we went over from Suttridge to give him a hand.'

'Good job you did, or you'd have had to spend your honeymoon haymaking,' said Tom seriously. Then he chuckled and added, 'That would have been a nice honeymoon for the pair of you.'

Bees were busy in the fragrant lime tree, and underneath a yew tree a thrush was tapping a snail on a stone. The grass in the churchyard was waist-high, ripening, and its heads drooping with seed.

'Fair crop of hay in here,' remarked Tom.

The air was still, not a leaf on the trees moved, the sky was cloudless. The sun, nearing its zenith, poured its heat down upon our shoulders. 'Going to be a scorcher,' said Tom. From the bright sunlight we stepped into the cool, dim porch, into the cooler musty interior of the church. Our footsteps echoed on the stone floor. Heads were turned to watch us walk slowly and self-consciously up the aisle to the chancel steps. We stood, staring at the altar, hands clasped behind our backs like a couple of naughty schoolboys sent to the front of the class. The altar and the lectern were decorated with white roses, delphiniums, and an abundance of moon daisies.

'Nothing to it really,' said Tom who so recently had stood where I stood now, waiting for his bride. Yet he, too, shuffled his feet as I did. Behind us we heard whispering, rustling and the sound of footsteps. Tom made feeble jokes, time seemed interminable. We decided we'd arrived too early, thus prolonging our ordeal.

I cautiously turned my head and saw Aunt Dorothea and my mother. Mother had a peculiar expression, she fiddled with her hair and flicked real or imaginary fluff from her clothes. Catching my eye, she gave an odd, embarrassed smile. My father looked as if he would rather be at home, sitting in his comfortable armchair and reading the *Daily Mail*. I half expected him to pull a copy from his pocket and shelter behind it. Aunt Dorothea was composed; no doubt a country wedding was a tame affair to the wife of a London bank manager.

Growing bolder, I turned and saw Aunt Aggie, my father's sister, and her husband Sam Fisher. Aggie was wearing her best black frock and a wide-brimmed hat with garish artificial cherries. She'd even put some rouge on her cheeks, badly applied and incongruous upon that mournful, pinched face. She smiled at me and her face looked even more mournful. Sam Fisher—I wondered how Aggie had persuaded him to come—was hunched in the pew, his sparse hair slicked down. With his drooping moustache and sagging eyes he looked thoroughly miserable. He clasped a bowler hat on his knees and the full-blown rose in his lapel looked as doleful as he did.

On the bride's side, the maiden aunts were in a state of excitement; heads bobbing, heads together. Old hands at weddings but never in the right rôle. Uncles stolid; cousins and second cousins, young and old, whispering, twittering, turning this way and that, missing nothing.

Mrs Peabody, my mother's great friend, was playing the organ and peeping round her screen from time to time. Mr Bence, the vicar, came from the vestry, looked at us all and returned. Uncle George arrived in his best tweed suit and wearing a large carnation. Proceeding up the aisle he stopped to speak to almost everyone, smiling, saying 'How d'ye do', or 'How nice to see you.' Grasping hands and shaking them vigorously, leaning over those nearest him to do the same thing to those at the far end of the pew. Having a more prolonged chat to his special friends, 'Got here then. That's the style. Nice morning for the job. You be well turned out. Makes you look years younger when you be done up a bit.'

The elder aunts had courteous attention—rather, I thought, to their consternation as he continued holding their hands. He sat down beside Aunt Aggie and said in a loud whisper, 'What-ho, Ag old girl. You be got up in fine style, and don't old Sam look a bobby-dazzler.' I turned away quickly, lest he should accost me in a loud voice. When I looked round later, he was running a finger round the inside of his stiff collar and tugging at it.

Mr Teakle limped into church. Up bounded Uncle George and rushed off to greet him, 'Well, well, Dan, b'ain't I glad to see you,' slapping him on the back and pushing him into a pew. 'We'll sit here, Dan,' he said.

A dozen or so village people came in and as they passed Uncle, he shot out an arm to shake them by the hand. Mother was turning round with a disapproving look, she whispered something to my father who stared pointedly in front of him. Mr and Mrs Clutterbuck arrived. Uncle George jumped up again and went down the aisle to meet them.

'Grand day for the job, ain't it?' he said as he shook them both by the hand, 'You look right spruce today, Arthur.' Pushing the usher aside, he showed them to a seat and sat down beside them. 'A good turn-out,' he observed, as he settled himself down. But he was on his feet the moment he saw Mr and Mrs Saggamore. 'Mornin', Ernest. Mornin', Martha. Got here then, Ernest, thought you wasn't goin' to make it. Bet Martha had a game to get you ready on time.' He gave them a slight push, 'In here,' he ordered and then squeezed in by them.

Mr Bence came from the vestry and spoke to Mrs Peabody at the organ. Molly's mother, elder sister and her husband walked to their seats. Uncle George greeted them quickly and then wandered around whispering and waving, as if to make sure that nobody had been missed out. Mr Bence, about to speak to me, observed his perambulations and scurried off to him. Uncle George returned to one of his many seats and Mr Bence walked towards the church doorway.

'Time's almost up,' whispered Tom. 'Want to try and make a run for it?'

Mr Bence hovered by the church door. Mrs Peabody kept glancing at him. Tom and I looked hard at the altar. Everyone, even Uncle George was quiet. Tom felt in his waistcoat pocket. Mrs Peabody started playing the Wedding March. Tom looked at his watch, 'Only four minutes late.'

I turned and saw Molly on her father's arm, walking towards us. She wore white lace and carried a bouquet of white roses and was followed by the bridesmaids in floral cotton voile and carrying bouquets of sweet peas. Molly was slowly coming towards me, she glanced at me and behind her veil I saw her wink—or did my eyes deceive me? Now Molly was at my side; a strange almost unapproachable Molly, all in white, while Mr Bence the vicar stood facing us.

'Dearly beloved, we are gathered here ... Therefore if any man can show any just cause why they may not lawfully be joined together ...' Mr Bence paused. What if someone did? I experienced a moment of tension, for no reason, but I always did at any wedding.

'Wilt thou have this woman ...?'

I heard myself say, 'I will.'

Then Mr Bence, (using the 1928 version which omits the promise to obey—Molly's and my choice), 'Wilt thou ...?'

In a small but very clear voice, Molly said, 'I will.'

Everything went well until I tried to slip the ring on to

Molly's finger. It wouldn't go on. I pushed and still it refused to go over her knuckle. It seemed as if the world had stopped. The whole congregation seemed to be holding its breath as I struggled desperately with that ring.

'Twist it. Twist it,' hissed the vicar.

I twisted and pushed, and twisted again. I seemed locked in an eternity, pushing and twisting at the ring and poor Molly's finger. Then suddenly, to my immense relief—and Molly's—it slipped on. Mr Bence smiled and continued with the service, the scent from the bridesmaids' bouquets wafted under my nose.

And equally suddenly it was all over. Mr Bence led us into the vestry. 'You may now kiss your wife,' he said to me and beamed at us both as I did so.

Soon Molly and I were walking down the aisle, arm in arm, stepping out of the cool porchway into the dazzling sun to face the world as man and wife.

When Molly and I came to the churchyard gates we found them closed and tied with rope. On the other side were half a dozen village people who demanded money before they opened the gates.

Soon we were standing with Molly's parents in the large room at The Crown, welcoming the guests. Molly's aunts flung their arms round her, hugged her and kissed her, and kissed me too. Her uncles shook me by the hand; some of them I'd met before, but most of them I was meeting for the first time.

'This is Uncle Clarence,' said Molly, as I shook the podgy hand of a short, tubby man.

'Nice to meet you,' squeaked Uncle Clarence, a thin voice, from a fat body. 'My word, you're sunburnt, Molly.'

Yes, Molly's sunburnt face looked very brown against the whiteness of her wedding dress and veil. Cousins and friends clustered in. And my father and mother; father rather subdued, I expect Mother had been making some tart

remarks about Uncle George's performance in church. Just
as she was moving away from us, she hissed, 'That George! I
could have died of shame.'

Aunt Aggie was effusive, she kissed Molly vigorously and
the cherries on her hat wobbled. 'You're one of the family
now,' she gushed. 'Here's your Uncle Sam.' Sam gave us a
weak smile and a nod. Jack Musgrove and Bill Lugg shuffled
in, looking strange and uncomfortable in blue suits and
without their caps. Uncle George kissed Molly gently on the
forehead. Mr and Mrs Saggamore, Mr Saggamore hesitant,
not knowing quite what to say or do.

Waitresses brought round trays of drink and food. Soon
everyone was busily eating, drinking and talking. I noticed
that Mr Saggamore and other farmers were in a huddle; they
were discussing farming.

I whispered to Molly, 'I thought you'd have been
nervous.'

'I was.'

'Well, you didn't look it. You actually winked.'

'Did I?' said Molly, wide eyed, 'I don't remember.'

'You've got lipstick all over your face.'

'Have I?' Molly dabbed her face with a handkerchief. 'It's
those old aunts. Father's sisters. They plaster it on themselves, they've no idea.'

Eventually the time came for Molly and I to cut the cake,
hand on hand. Corks popped, bottles of champagne and
glasses were taken round by the waitresses. Mr Clutterbuck
made a gentle, touching little speech. Tom made a short,
competent speech, and I made a bumbling one.

'Hah,' said Mr Clutterbuck, when all that was over, 'do
you remember when you were too shy to ask Molly to go to
the concert with you?'

'Oh, I never knew that,' exclaimed my mother.

'And do you remember what day it was?' continued Mr
Clutterbuck.

Yes, I remembered. It was St Valentine's Day, but I'd thought it just coincidence.

Everyone was chatting away. Molly was laughing at something Tom had said.

'Hold hard!' cried Uncle George rising from his chair in an ungainly manner. 'Hold hard, I haven't spoken yet.' His voice was loud, everyone stopped talking and turned to look at him. 'I b'ain't goin' to let this occasion pass without sayin' somethin'. Old Arthur Clutterbuck didn't make a bad job of what he said, but t'ain't adequate, if you get my meanin'. What I mean is, you gotta make a proper job on't.' He paid Molly some pretty compliments. He dealt at great length on her virtues, quite unconscious of how confused and embarrassed he was making her. Uncle George rambled on and on. Pigs, plums, apples, cabbages, cider, all crept into his discourse. Molly looked puzzled and I whispered to her, 'Parsnip wine', knowing that Uncle fortified himself with parsnip wine before any 'occasion'. I could see Mother, tight-lipped, nudging Father. Aunt Dorothea looked disdainful. Aunt Aggie was attentive and Sam Fisher was busily eating, taking no notice of anybody.

Molly's mother seemed amused. Her father and some of her aunts were smiling, others seemed puzzled. The Aunt, who'd confessed to a 'funny feeling', hiccoughed loudly and her face reddened. Molly's uncles looked sleepy; Uncle Clarence had dozed off and was snoring. The cousins were giggling and chattering. Most of the local people just sat solid and impassive.

Happy, flushed, and gently sweating, Uncle George paused to mop his brow. And then, looking puzzled, he said, 'Now, where was I? I've forgotten what I was agoin' to say. 'Old on a minute, 'ave another drink while I 'ave a ponder. Drink to the bride an' groom. It'll all come back to me directly. Good health to the happy couple. Me nephew's a lucky young feller, havin' a wife like young Molly. I wish

I'd got married, but it's too late now. Wish I'd done it years ago, but I was allus so busy. Never 'ad the time y'know, allus 'ad so much to do, what with one thing an' another.'

Uncle mopped his brow again. My mother was glaring and digging an elbow into Father. Aunt Aggie looked blissful, Uncle Sam's eyes looked a bit glassy. Molly's father was whispering to his wife.

'Let's drink to the happy couple again,' said Uncle George. 'Me nephew ain't such a bad young chap neither, which ain't s'prisin' seein' as I've 'ad the 'andlin' of 'im since 'e were knee 'igh to a grasshopper. So 'ere's to their health and happiness and may the years be kind to 'em. There, I be about finished now.'

But ten minutes later he was on his feet again. 'Ain't the bride's father goin' to say summat?' he asked. Molly's father declined. 'I should 'ave thought the bride's father would 'ave said a few words. Well, what about you, Ernest, be you goin' to say summat? No, well what about you, Daniel? You be a pretty little speaker, you'll say summat an' to the point I'll warrant. No? What's the matter with you all? C'mon vicar, you'll say a few words.'

'No,' replied Mr Bence, 'I don't think there's any need.'

'In that case. I'll say a bit more', said Uncle George, 'to put the finishin' touch to the occasion, unless the boy's father'll do't.'

'If you don't,' Mother hissed to Father, giving him a prod, 'the cratur will go on for ever.'

'No, Ethel. I'll make a proper haggle of it. You know that,' murmured Father.

Molly's father jumped up. Smiling all round, but particularly at Uncle George, he said, 'Sir, you have delighted us long enough. You have said all that need be said, and we must allow these two young people to go and change now or they'll miss their train.'

CHAPTER FIVE

Last days at Suttridge

After our honeymoon we lived with my parents. We would move to Perrygrove Farm, that 'little place just over yonder' at Michaelmas. Molly and I both longed for Michaelmas to come; we hadn't much chance to learn to live together while we were with my parents. During the day Molly still worked at Willow Farm, and I at Suttridge. At night when we went to bed there was just a hint of embarrassment. My mother made us feel we shouldn't be going to bed together; she would look very uneasy as we said good night. We slept in the double bed which had been in the spare room; the bed which Aunt Dorothea had slept in when she visited us. I daresay the bed had done well enough for her, but for newly weds, no. 'Can't you do something about the springs? I feel sure your mother is listening for every creak, couldn't you oil them or something?' Molly asked me.

It was a far more trying time for Molly than for me, and it says much for her that she managed to remain reasonably good tempered, at least in my mother's presence. 'I hope you manage to cook all right when you're on your own, he's very fussy about his food,' my mother would say. And any offers from Molly to help with the cooking brought a curt 'No thank you'.

I did think Molly was near breaking point when I heard Mother had said to her, 'I think your underwear is hardly suitable for a married woman, dear. You should wear something more substantial, like me.' 'That's what your mother said to me', Molly told me angrily, 'but if she thinks I'm going about in those baggy old bloomers like her, she's mistaken.' And then, I overheard Mother saying to her, 'If you must wear those scanty things, you must dry them in your room. I can't have Father seeing them on my line, they're never decent.'

She continued nagging Molly to take me to church, and even offered to accompany us. She tried again and again to get Molly to join the Women's Institute. 'It would be so good for you, dear. You'd learn so much and get to know a lot of people.'

'Does that woman think that I know nothing?' snorted Molly when we were alone. 'Does she think I have nothing better to do than spend my time at meetings with a lot of women? Anyway, I can't stand all-female company. All women together—and I expect all men together—brings out the worst. The sexes shouldn't be separated, it's all wrong. And that's another thing, I happened to use the word sex, and your mother said, in that shocked way of hers, "Don't ever use that word dear, it's not nice." And she also objects to the word breast, "say chest, dear, it's so much nicer."

52

And then this morning she says it's a pity I don't wear a corset. I told her to hell with corsets and she didn't like it, but I don't care. And you can tell her that I don't care, if you like.'

Father, wisely I thought, kept quiet during Mother's conversations about church, Women's Institute and other matters, but Molly thought otherwise. 'Why doesn't your father speak? I'm sick of him just sitting there and never saying a word. It makes me feel most uncomfortable. I really can't help thinking what a peculiar family yours is!'

Molly was careful not to become embroiled in Mother's constant bickering about my father's brother George, and his sister Aggie, although Mother tried hard to enlist her sympathy and possible support.

Aunt Aggie had promised us a chest of drawers. 'Don't bring the thing back here,' said Mother. 'I don't want it here, it's bound to be all worm-eaten if that Aggie's giving it away. I don't want it here infesting my furniture.'

'From what I hear', said Father, 'it's that chest that belonged to my mother. If it is—and our George says it is, and he's bound to be right—it's a beautiful piece of furniture. You don't get craftsmanship like that today.'

'Huh,' snorted Mother, 'I've never known that Aggie to give anything away that's worth having.'

'Solid oak, with brass handles, lovely bit of craftsmanship. My mother used to polish it every day. She used to keep our place like a palace. On from morning to night, she was.'

'Oh!' said Mother, her neck going red, 'meaning that I don't. You're criticising me now, are you? After all I've done for you.'

'Now, now, old lady,' soothed Father. I thought Molly was going to laugh, but she managed to keep a straight face. 'I just thought it was nice of Aggie, giving them the chest. It must be worth a tidy bit,' continued Father, 'and as for critting you, I wouldn't dream on't. Our George is always saying what a master cook you be.'

'That's all you ever think of is your stomach, and as for that George, he's nothing but stomach,' retorted Mother. She turned to Molly. 'If I'd only known what I know now, I'd never have got married. When I was a girl I wanted to go into a convent, but my people talked me out of it. I used to be a Sunday School teacher and I went to church three times on a Sunday, and most days I went into the church to say a prayer. They said I'd got religious mania, they even took me to the doctor, and bought me a bicycle.'

'Our George says—' began Father.

But Mother cut in quickly, saying to Molly, 'You've been here long enough now to see what I've got to put up with. Always having that George rammed down my neck and the cratur everlasting here. Many's the time I've put on my hat and coat and threatened to leave, never to return.'

'You'd better get off to your Aunt's for that chest,' said Father.

Sam Fisher was slumped in a deep armchair when we arrived. Sam had been retired for some years. Once he'd been slim, lethargic and lugubrious, now he was fat, almost immobile and morose. Aggie was as thin as ever and still clothed in black. But despite her dismal appearance she had a sense of humour.

'Here are our visitors, Sam,' said Aunt Aggie, with a false attempt at brightness. Sam, head in hands, did not speak or stir. Aggie tried again, 'Aren't you going to speak to them?' There was a slight movement of his head and not a twitch of his shoulders. Aggie whispered to us, 'It's not one of his good days.'

'Aargh,' grunted Sam.

'It's his head,' whispered Aunt Aggie. 'The poor old fella's

54

head's playing him up, it's because of all that shifty work in the factory during the war and the metal fatigue, he's never really got over it.' In a louder voice she said, 'I'll make a nice cup of tea, and when you've had that and a couple of aspirins you'll feel better. Would you like a little drop of brandy first?'

'Aargh.'

'I give him a drop, just for medicinal reasons,' explained Aunt Aggie. Uncle George had told us that Sam had several drops of brandy every day since he'd had a little legacy.

Aunt Aggie handed him a glass containing brandy. 'Here you are, old fellow, drink this.' She then handed him a packet of Woodbines. 'Have a ciggy while I put the kettle on.'

Sam took the brandy and the cigarettes in a grudging manner and after drinking the brandy in one gulp he poked a cigarette into his mouth. Aggie flitted over to the mantelshelf for a box of matches and she lit his cigarette. Sam puffed, but gave no word or sign of thanks.

While Aunt Aggie was out of the room, Molly spoke to Sam. 'It's lovely weather, Mr Fisher.'

'Aargh,' muttered Sam and slowly turned his head to the window. In silence he gazed sullenly at the sunshine and at the butterflies fluttering around the buddleia. 'We shall pay for it later,' he said at last. 'We'll have a hard winter, I shouldn't doubt.'

'Oh, I hope not!' exclaimed Molly, 'I hope our first winter at Perrygrove isn't a difficult one.'

'Never did like farming,' said Sam, the cigarette still between his lips and dropping ash on his cardigan, the end in his mouth now brown and soggy. 'Too much hard work, too many disappointments, animals allus dying, crops failing or being ruined by the weather. Ah, I've seen more than one go bust at farming.'

Aunt Aggie returned with the tea tray. She took Sam's cigarette end and flung it into the fireplace and brushed the ash from his cardigan with her hand before handing him a cup of tea and two aspirins. Sam put the aspirins into his mouth, poured tea into his saucer and sucked at it. As we left the room Aggie asked him if he felt better. 'No,' he replied, almost with satisfaction.

The chest of drawers, which she took us upstairs to see, was a nice piece of furniture, made of oak and with splendid brass handles—and without a trace of woodworm. Molly and I were delighted, but our delight couldn't equal Aunt Aggie's. Her face was a paroxysm of pleasure and tiny tears glistened in the corners of her eyes.

My last weeks at Suttridge were spent with conflicting desires, eager to be away and yet reluctant to leave; the former the stronger, but I'd grown fond of Suttridge, its fields and streams, its trees and hedges. Harvest that year proceeded apace with our own combine. As soon as the ripe, standing corn was dry enough in the morning, when the dew had left the plump drooping ears, we started combining and continued until dusk. When the driver of the combine and the man with him bagging the corn stopped for food, others took their places and the combining proceeded without a break. Those not busy on the combine loaded the full sacks of corn on a trailer and took them to the barn, and the straw was baled and stacked.

The machines made harvesting easier and quicker and yet time seemed more precious than ever, not a moment to lose. The machine did not tire, and man worked to its tempo. The machine was his master.

Gone was the reaping, stooking, loading and unloading of wagons; the careful stacking, thatching, and the threshing later. And gone with these was something of the joy and rhythm of harvest work, and the pride and romance of the harvest. No longer the comradeship of shared work. Little now of the slow, steady talk, the reminiscences and the oft repeated and much loved old jokes. The speed and the noise precluded these delights, and we didn't all sit together by stack or wagon wheel at meal times. Bird song and rustle of straw were drowned by the roar of machinery. And at the end of the day, instead of the satisfying tiredness of aching muscle and weary arm, there was a dull stupefying fatigue. No longer a jingle of chains as horses went to the stable, a stumbling iron shod hoof striking the cobbles. When at last the machines stopped, the sudden silence seemed strange.

The combine had disadvantages. The corn was often damp and couldn't be easily stored and this meant a sudden glut of corn on the market. With stacks of course, this didn't happen—the corn being threshed and sold during the winter months.

The other disadvantage with combines was the weed seed which it threw out on the fields. With the older method of harvesting the majority of weed seed was carted with the corn and destroyed after threshing. Weed sprays were becoming popular to deal with the problem, but this meant more money being spent on sprays and sprayers and once again the farmer was relying on scientists and factories.

But there were gains as well as losses. The main joy now was in getting the job done as opposed to the job itself. There was a satisfaction in beating the weather and in getting the crop safely harvested. There is no pleasure, whatever the method of harvesting, in seeing a crop ruined by storm. If conditions are such that sufficient men cannot or will not work the land, full advantage must be made of machines.

And while Jack in the factory (or Jack in office) is more highly regarded and highly paid than Jack in the field, such conditions will prevail. But man belongs to the land and to the land man must and will return. 'Land', Mr Saggamore said to me years ago, 'is the honestest thing.' And so it is, and more. It is the source of life and the foundation of all culture. If mankind is to survive, the land must be served.

Ernest Saggamore lived farming, breathed farming; he thought farming all day and probably dreamed farming all night. And therein lay his success, for farming is a jealous, all demanding taskmaster. Often I've had cause to reproach myself, catching myself dreaming, letting my thoughts wander. Idling, watching the sunlight on an oak tree, studying the dappled sunlight beneath. Lingering to gaze at a flower in the hedgerow when I should have been busy about my business. And yet Mr Saggamore also noticed the wild flowers and had time to hear and watch the skylark overhead. Some, not all, of the old time farmers were romantics at heart, though they'd have been shocked if they'd been told so. Why else did they take such pains to see that furrows were ploughed and corn drilled so straight, take such a pride in a well laid hedge? This applied to many a farmworker too. And I've seen many a tough, shrewd, tightfisted old farmer bid an extra five or ten pounds for a cow, just because she was a pretty animal.

Little escaped Saggamore's notice, his observation was keen. It is a trait a farmer must have or acquire. The animal standing slightly apart from the herd or flock, the one that is just a little bit slow in coming for its food; having that hunched or tucked-up look, be it only just apparent. Dull coat or eyes, dung not quite normal. In farming more than most things, a stitch in time saves nine.

As in sight, so in sound; the farmer, even when abed, must sleep with one ear open. There may be several different noises in the farmyard during the night; the bellowing cow for the calf taken from her, and the calf, raucous because it's been taken from its mother; the sound of a cow in distress at calving. All these and many more, the farmer must be able to differentiate between them and to know if an animal needs his attention. Gradually, you learn.

'The farmer's foot is the best dung,' Mr Saggamore said. 'Stop on your farm and see to your own business, that'll do more good than looking to the government for help.' Much of his success was due to being 'well forward with the seasonable work. Never put off till tomorrow what you can do today'.

'Remember,' he told me, during my last weeks with him, 'the less you spend, the less you have to make.' During the last few years he had bought a couple of tractors, a pick-up baler, and a combine. And though he could well afford it he kept saying, 'We'll have to steady up, or we'll be ruined.' As more farmers went over to specialised dairy farming, he shook his head and said, 'their ground will get cow sick, they'll have trouble later. Milking a lot of cows is all right when its going all right, but it never does for long. Mixed farming is the best farming.'

This was the time when dairy farmers were vying with each other to produce higher and higher yields of milk. 'It isn't the amount of milk in the bucket that's important, it's how much that is really yours that counts,' said Saggamore, who never blindly followed the prevailing fashion. Heavy application of fertilisers was also becoming fashionable and though Saggamore used them, he used them judiciously.

'Artificials are all right,' he told me one day, slapping a bag as was often his custom when making a pronouncement, 'but they ain't got any residual value, you've got to have dung as well. Dunging the land's like putting money in the bank and using artificial's like withdrawing it, and we all know what happens if you keep withdrawing money and never deposit any.'

Suttridge was always well cropped and stocked, but he warned me of the peril of overstocking. 'When you're short of fodder, everybody else is, and you're at the mercy of the market—a seller's market and you're a buyer. A spare rick of hay will always pay the rent of the ground it stands on, it's like having money in the bank.'

Yet, in the years to come these maxims were ignored, scorned, and the very opposite put into effect. But not immediately. The nature of our countryside acted as a bulwark against 'big business farming'.

Bill's brother, Gritton, was now a full-time employee at Suttridge. He would replace me as cowman when I left. Gritton thought highly of himself as a cowman and as a mechanic too. He could hold the sparking plugs of a tractor while it was running. 'You'll never be a mechanic', he told us, 'until you can do that.'

'Bless my soul,' said Jack, his face as straight as could be; if you didn't know Jack, you'd think he was taking it all in, 'I never knowed that.'

'Yes, that's right,' said Gritton sharply, his eyes shining, 'that's the test of a good tractor driver.'

'By gum', said Bill, 'then I'll have a go, aye I will.' And Bill, ever ready to display his skill with tractors, grasped two of the sparking plugs. 'Oh! Bloody hell!' he exclaimed, bounding backwards. 'They'm bloody fierce, aye, them be. They'm a bloody sight 'otter than wasps fit, aye 'em be.'

'I'd aim it do take some time to learn skills like that, Grit,' observed a very serious Jack.

'Just a gift,' replied Gritton nonchalantly, 'either you've got it or you ain't.'

Previously, when Gritton had only worked occasionally at Suttridge, he and Bill had been great friends. Bill regarded his brother as an authority on almost everything. 'Our Grit do know, aye 'im do', was a remark we'd frequently heard from Bill. 'Our Grit'll know, aye 'im 'ull. I'll ask our Grit, aye I 'ull.' Though Bill was the elder, he deferred to Gritton, Bill being by nature an underdog and Gritton the reverse. But even underdogs when driven to it will rebel and Bill sometimes quarrelled with his brother. Once with pitchforks; and Jack who had to intervene remarked later, 'There ain't goin' to be a dull moment here, with them two silly b's about.'

'I'm not havin' fightin' and quarrellin' here,' stated Mr Saggamore. Actually, the brothers never quarrelled in his presence, but little happened at Suttridge without his being aware of it. Despite all the wiggings he gave him, Mr Saggamore was fond of Bill, and guessing that Gritton was the culprit he threatened him with dismissal if the quarrelling continued.

'If he sacks our Grit, I'll leave'n, aye I 'ull,' muttered Bill. 'If he gives our Grit his cards, I'll ask fer mine, aye, I 'ull.'

'If he sacks me,' Gritton told Jack and me, with a sharp look in his eyes, 'I'll have the union on him, I will. I'll pull him. I'll pull him, that I will.' Gritton was a keen union man and frequenty exhorted Jack to join, but Jack was unenthusiastic.

'If you die the union'll bury you, Jack, aye 'em 'ull,' said Bill, backing up his brother.

'That's the least of my worries, getting buried,' retorted Jack. 'I'd aim as I'll get buried all right, if they don't bury me 'cos they love me, they'll bury me 'cos I stink.'

Some farmers tried and some succeeded, to prevent their men joining the union but Saggamore didn't care if they joined or not, it was a matter of indifference to him. If a worker did his job that was all that mattered. Bill and Gritton settled down together well enough. Gritton knew as well as anybody that Mr Saggamore would have no qualms about sacking him. Saggamore's great strength was his independence; he would have done his usual work and Gritton's as well if necessary. To Saggamore no one was indispensable, he'd simply do the work himself. 'That's

61

where the boss have got everybody beat,' Jack once said. 'He could and would do it himself, he ain't no ordinary man.'

During my last month at Suttridge I went to see Mr Bishop, the auctioneer, about the in-going valuation at Perrygrove Farm.

'Mr Bishop has had to go out,' said the middle-aged woman, looking at me over large horn-rimmed spectacles, 'but he won't be long. Perhaps you'd like to wait in the office.'

She took me down a narrow passage, its varnished wooden panelling cracked and dark with age. At the end of the passage she turned the handle of a door and pushed the door open with an outstretched arm, standing aside for me to enter the office. 'He shouldn't be more than five minutes, he is expecting you,' she said slowly, half an apology, half in explanation. And then, briskly, 'Now if you'll excuse me, I'll get on with my work.'

The door closed and I heard the tap of her high heels along the passage. I sat down in a wooden armchair in front of a large roll-topped desk, and in a few moments heard the clatter and ring of a typewriter.

It was a warm, mellow morning in early September, and yet, despite the richness and the warmth of the morning, there was already the first faint feeling of autumn. The sun slanted through the window on my left and a wasp buzzed and muddled languidly in the corner of a window pane. The balmy air, the sun—specks of dust caught in its rays—and the wasp gave the office a drowsy, limpid atmosphere, its tranquillity broken only by the vigorous chatter of the typewriter next door.

A grey bowler hat and a couple of light coloured raincoats hung on a big cumbersome wooden hat stand in the corner near the doorway, and beside this stood a large old fashioned bookcase filled with reference books and box files. Behind the desk was a fireplace, its elaborate ironwork and tiled surrounds encrusted with soot. Over the fireplace hung a large print, framed and glazed, of a horse and rider. Flanking it were photographs of fat Shorthorn bullocks, winners of Christmas fatstock shows possibly; and of long ago judging by the dress of the men proudly standing by the animals. On the other walls were some Alken sporting prints and notices of farm sales.

One of these sale notices in particular caught my attention. WILLOW FARM. K. DENT BISHOP & SONS HAVE BEEN KINDLY FAVOURED WITH THE INSTRUCTIONS OF ARTHUR CLUTTERBUCK ESQ., TO SELL BY AUCTION THE WHOLE LIVE AND DEAD FARMING STOCK WITHOUT RESERVE. The livestock consisted of the complete herd of old-established and deep-milking Shorthorn cattle, various bunches of grand Hereford cross store cattle, a flock of Suffolk sheep, several Gloucester Old Spot pigs close to farrowing, various lots of poultry, and four Shire horses, quiet, and good workers in all gears.

The deadstock was stock that had never been livestock; wagons, carts, ploughs and other implements, dairy equipment and tools. And several lots of valuable household furniture would be sold. The sale *would*, said the notice, *commence at 11.30 a.m. prompt.* But anyone with experience of farm sales knew that 'prompt' was a vain hope. Even at twelve it would require some frantic ringing of hand-bells to get the farmers assembled for the sale of the first lots.

Short sharp footsteps coming down the passage ended my reverie. The door opened very quickly and in stepped Mr Bishop. A short, thick-set man; around sixty, and florid of face. Perched on his head was a grey bowler hat. Tiny beads of sweat stood on his forehead.

'Good morning, good morning,' he said, in a quick rather breathless voice. I started to rise. 'No, don't get up. Sorry

63

I'm late. Blasted hot this morning' he said, and started to mop his face with a spotted blue handkerchief.

He was wearing a bright checked jacket, a canary yellow waistcoat, and narrow black and white checked trousers. He looked, as indeed he was, a colourful man both in character and dress. He hung his walking stick on the hat-stand then sat down behind his desk, the hat still perched on his head. He placed his short stubby fingers on the edge of the desk and looked straight at me with clear blue eyes. 'Aha', he said and cleared his throat, 'Aha,' and cleared his throat again.

He beat a rapid tattoo on his desk top causing me to notice a gold ring and well manicured fingers. 'I've got it all fixed up.' His rapid, breathless speech, as if he'd got to speak quickly before his breath expired. He mopped his brow again before saying, 'Bit of a job, fitting it in. Busy time of year for we fellers.' A forefinger pushed his hat back an inch. 'Farm sales—um, um, um,'—up went the finger and back went the hat—'But Rolls and I can fix your valuation in. We can manage October 16th.' Rolls was a partner in the auctioneering firm who would be doing the outgoing valuation.

'All seems straightforward, shouldn't be any bother. If we can't agree I know a good feller we can call in to arbitrate, name of Kerr. Shrewd feller, shrewd feller.' Mr Bishop cleared his throat again, then continued in that husky tone. Only slightly breathless now, and I noticed that when he spoke at length, he spoke much slower. 'Might have to call in Kerr. Kerr's a very good feller y'know.' He picked up a pencil and opened a notebook. 'There's the stuff you'll want to take—to, hay—you know, consumable stores. Barbed wire around the farm. A helluva fiddle, you'll be surprised how it mounts up. Unexhausted manurial residues, there'll be something to pay on that. Then there's the stuff they'll want you to take, we'll need to be careful there.' He read out several items from a list in his notebook. We discussed them

64

briefly and then he said, 'I think we'd better pop over in a day or two and have a look.'

He rummaged in the litter on his desk and eventually produced a diary. After studying it he looked up, 'I could manage next Wednesday. All right for you?' He asked me a few questions and as I answered he tapped the desk with a pencil. 'Shouldn't think', he said, closing his notebook, 'there'll be any dilapidations, Barnard's a tidy enough feller from all I've heard tell.' Barnard was the outgoing tenant. 'Not that you want any dilapidations today,' he said, using the point of his pencil to push his hat back still further. 'Cost far more to put 'em right than ever you'd get in compensation.'

After a moment's cogitation, Mr Bishop said quietly to himself, as if I was not present, 'Times are changing, it's the end of the old ways. They'll never see what I and my kind have seen, nor men like we have known. But we're old, of course we're old, and like the old ways we're going. Old Simmonds went last month, and who'll go next? But 'tis in the nature of things, a time to sow and a time to reap.' He looked up, aware again of my presence. 'Yes, we're going, going, and new men are coming to the land. You'll see a very different farming, young man. But you've been taught by one of the old sort, you'll be proud of that one day.'

I thought it was time for me to leave, but suddenly Mr Bishop flung down his pencil, jumped to his feet, pulled his gold watch from his waistcoat pocket and studied it with a furrowed brow. 'Ahem! Ahem! Well, come on then, we'll pop round to The Lamb.' He pulled his hat forward and grabbed his walking stick. We stopped at the glass fronted door halfway along the passage, and poking his head round the doorway he said to the woman I'd met earlier, 'If anybody calls, tell them I've had to go out.'

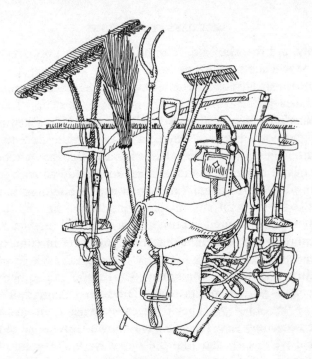

CHAPTER SIX

Mr Clutterbuck's Sale

My impending departure and the tender September sun lent enchantment to Suttridge; to her fields of newly turned furrows, to the low-lying meadows where the cows stood swishing their tails under the pollarded willows, to the pastures where the sleek Hereford cattle grazed and the flock of breeding ewes, their fleeces still snowy white. Forgotten were the days of boredom and drudgery, the days of mud and slush; the back-breaking days of root hoeing or sugar beet hauling.

As Mr Clutterbuck's sale approached I'd imagined he'd be in a sombre frame of mind. So, I was surprised to find him lighthearted, almost jocular when I met him in The

66

Crown a few days before the sale. True, his sagging jowls still sagged, his rubicund face was still careworn and his shoulders still drooped, but his eyes looked brighter than I'd ever seen them.

'Now it's come to, I'm glad,' he told me. 'I'd been putting it off for years, but now I'm glad. I feel a sense of relief, the farm has been getting too much for me. I've got worn out like an old horse. I've suddenly realised I've had enough of getting up at five-thirty every morning, of cold, dark, wet mornings.'

Mr Clutterbuck like others of his age was an early riser. A habit borne of the days when horses had to be fed early in the morning to be ready for a day's work in the fields; when the milk had to be at the station in time for the early milk train. The tractor, and the Milk Marketing Board, with its lorries collecting milk at the farm, had changed all that. But Mr Clutterbuck never had a tractor; and what's more, he and his kind did not lightly cast aside tradition and the habits of a lifetime.

'And it'll be better for the missus', said Mr Clutterbuck slowly, 'not having that big house to worry about. I don't know how either of us would have managed this last few years without young Molly.'

Mr Clutterbuck lapsed into silence—a silence I hesitated to break—and gazed vacantly in that manner peculiar to old men. 'Ah,' he said at last, as if he'd returned from a long journey, 'you've a good wife there.' I felt a sense of gratitude towards Mr Clutterbuck. If it hadn't been for him I'd never have met Molly. Also, I suspected he'd had a hand in my getting Perrygrove.

We were standing against the bar and Mr Clutterbuck pulled a half-crown out of his pocket and slid it across the counter. When Trophimus Ellicot, the publican, had refilled our glasses, Mr Clutterbuck raised his with, 'Here's luck to you.' And then, in measured tones, 'And

you'll need it. You'll have a struggle, I've had one all my
life, farming's a gamble. There's the weather, good seasons
and bad, disease and sheer bad luck, we must expect all that
and learn to cope with it as best we can. But the bugbear of
farming is the politicians, they play shuttlecock with farming. To hear some of 'em talk, you'd think farming's going
to be all right for ever and ever. Guaranteed markets and
prices, the Agricultural Act. We had the Corn Production
Act after the first war and they repealed it. And they'll
repeal this one when it suits 'em. I can see the writing on the
wall, that's another reason why I'm getting out. You know,
it's a terrible thing that it takes a war to put farming on its
feet.'

Mr Clutterbuck pulled a gold watch from his waistcoat
pocket; holding it in the palm of his hand he studied it
intently for a second or two. 'Well,' he said, slipping the
watch back into his pocket, 'I must be getting back to the
missus.'

We left The Crown together. Molly had been to Perrygrove to measure the windows and I'd left her busily making
curtains at home.

Fortunately for Mr Clutterbuck the weather was fine for his
sale. A warm day and a nice bit of sun always showed the
animals to advantage and it put prospective purchasers in
good humour. Farm sales usually attracted a large gathering
and the sale at Willow Farm was no exception.

Farmers from miles away were there as well as local
farmers. Several of their wives had also come and were
examining the furniture for sale, or standing about in little
knots gossiping. Village people, and a few farmworkers
wandered around. A farm sale was regarded as a day out by
many. A chance to see what was for sale, a chance to see the
farm buildings—and for the women, if they were lucky, an

opportunity to see over the house. Above all, it was a good time for meeting friends and neighbours.

Among the many come to view and the few to buy was the usual contingent of those perhaps best described as 'hangers-on'. Most of them were of shabby appearance, some were downright dirty. They had come to gaze, to poke and prod or kick, or to make comments. Some were small time dealers hoping to pick up a bargain or two; most of these regarded themselves as very sharp fellows indeed. Their nods and winks and sly looks were all part of the game they were playing. Always hopeful of getting something for nothing, or practically nothing, of a clever deal, of putting 'a sharp one over' someone.

Uncle George's friends, Reuben Kimmins and Colonel Biggs—Colonel being only a nickname—were there. Reuben and Colonel were likeable, but rather disreputable. Reuben was a jobbing builder and recently Colonel had teamed up with him. On the strength of a small joint win on the football pools they'd bought a little battered old van and painted on its sides: KIMMINS & BIGGS, HIGH CLASS BUILDERS. They didn't do much trade, although there was plenty of work about. Jobbing builders were in demand and Reuben was quite a good tradesman, but most of the time they could find more interesting, if less lucrative, things to do. Drinking, talking, poaching, looking for a bargain, messing about; they were a happy-go-lucky pair, and their little windfall had given them the means, temporarily at least, to indulge in their favourite pastimes. They'd indulged in them before they'd had the means and undoubtedly still would long after the means had vanished.

Jack Musgrove and Bill Lugg had been sent to help with the animals. Gritton had been left at Suttridge and had showed his jealousy in a bout of bad temper before they left. 'I were durned glad to get from our Grit this morning. 'Im didn't 'alf 'ave it on 'im, aye 'im did,' Bill told me. Bill had been in disgrace the day before. He'd driven the new tractor over some spike harrows, puncturing its large, water-ballasted rear wheels.

'God Almighty!' Mr Saggamore had roared. 'There's water shooting forty foot up into the air! That little job'll cost me a packet. That old muntle'll be the ruination of me yet.'

Bill could offer no satisfactory explanation of why or how the accident had happened, and even if he'd been able to Mr Saggamore wouldn't have been in the mood to listen.

'I can't understand it, no I can't. I was just driving along and whoosh! There 'twas, aye it was,' mumbled Bill.

'Whoosh be buggered! It's whoosh all right and I'll whoosh you too,' threatened Mr Saggamore, his arms wildly flailing.

'It's a mystery,' mumbled Bill.

'It's no mystery to me,' snapped Mr Saggamore. 'You knew the harrows was there, but you weren't looking. Got that damned fag in yer mouth and smoke in yer eyes and you just don't think or care. I don't know what I shall do with you. You'll ruin me.'

Later I heard Mr Saggamore telling Jack all about it, waving his arms as he spoke. 'Forty foot in the air, Jack. Water shooting forty foot and two new tyres ruined. No farm'll ever stand jobs like that for long. What's come over him do you think, Jack? Have he gone off his head or summat? He's shaking like a leaf, it have scared him. I only hope it'll be a lesson to the muntle.'

But today at the sale Bill was cheerful; yesterday was yesterday and he soon forgot his troubles. His weather-beaten face, the colour of a walnut fresh from its husk, was creased in smiles, He'd borrowed a white smock for the occasion, and a mouldy old bowler hat which perched, rather ridiculously, on his round head. 'Where did you get that hat, Bill?' several people asked.

'Whatever have you got that hat on for, Bill?' asked Mr Saggamore, scathingly.

'Our Grit said it was the proper thing to wear in the sale ring, aye 'im did,' answered Bill, smiling from ear to ear.

'Well, take it off, everybody's laughing at you,' growled Mr Saggamore, turning on his heel.

Bill's face dropped, he flung the hat down and gave it a vicious kick. As I hurried after Mr Saggamore, I heard him mutter, 'I can't do nothin' right, no I can't. If Jack wore a bloody jerry on his 'ead it'd be all right, aye it 'ould.'

The auction started half an hour later than the advertised time. Mr Bishop and a clerk clambered on to an improvised rostrum, and Walter, Mr Clutterbuck's man trotted the horses up and down. Mr Clutterbuck, pipe in mouth, stood by the rostrum and watched them being sold; the smoke from his pipe curling upwards in the still air, a sombre expression on his face. No one was surprised at the low prices the horses realised.

The Dairy Shorthorns were not expected to make much either, dual-purpose cows were becoming increasingly unfashionable. And so for that matter was beef production; most farmers were keeping more milking cows, especially now that it was so easy to milk them with machines.

Mr Saggamore and I stood side by side as Walter ushered the first cow into the makeshift sale ring. We'd examined the cows prior to the sale, and elicited information about them from Mr Clutterbuck, Molly, and from Walter. We knew which cows I should try and buy, and had put a tentative price on them. The first five cows were old, 'you don't want them, they're too old,' Mr Saggamore had said. Neither did anyone else and they were all sold cheaply to a dealer. The next cow, one I'd marked in my catalogue, made much more than we'd expected and so did the next, causing some surprise among the local farmers. It wasn't the local men who were doing the spirited bidding, but strangers.

'Ha,' said Mr Saggamore, with some satisfaction, 'they ain't all gone in for black and whites.' And then in undertones to me he added, 'I'm afraid you'll have to spring another tenner or more.'

Encouraged by Mr Saggamore, I managed to buy the next cow; a nice roan, freshly calved, her distended udder dripping milk. Bringing the palm of his hand down slap, Mr Bishop shouted my name. That's a great moment for any young farmer, the first time an auctioneer calls out his name without having to ask for it.

Then the cow's muzzled heifer calf was brought into the ring. 'Don't,' appealed Mr Bishop, looking straight at me, 'part mother and daughter.' I bought the calf, not only because I wanted it, but I wasn't going to start my farming career by parting mother from daughter. Exhilarated, I bid for several more cows, purchasing another three, until cautioned by Mr Saggamore. Buying at an auction is intoxicating and it's so easy to become reckless. 'Let it go at that, you've got four cows. Better to buy some of the bulling heifers or yearlings,' he advised, 'they're always the cheapest class of stock to buy. They won't cost much to keep and they'll soon grow into profit. Besides, they've got all their lives in front of 'em.'

Walter and Jack Musgrove drove the bulling heifers in pairs into the ring. Not so docile as the cows, they were startled by the crowd. 'Whoa-up, my beauties,' soothed Walter as they tried to jump the ring. 'There's health and life and beauty; what more do you want?' cried Mr Bishop.

'Slip a bid in quick for that pair,' hissed Mr Saggamore. Mr Bishop shouted my name again, and I bought the following pair too.

Mr Saggamore bought some of the store cattle. 'Cattle always do well from this place,' he said. Some of the small-time dealers put in bids for the stores, but they dropped out when the bidding rose to a reasonable figure.

Their antics and subterfuges were amusing to watch. Unlike Mr Saggamore and most other farmers, they didn't stand boldly by the sale ring but dodged about, hiding first one side of the auctioneer and then the other, and tugging at his coat or trousers when they wished to register a bid. Or dodging round the outside of the ring behind other people, and cautiously waving a hand or stick before slinking off to some other position. It was all part of their trade, their supposed cunning; nobody should know they were bidding. In their minds they thought that if others saw them bidding—they who knew a thing or two—everyone would bid, thinking they were on to a good thing.

When it came to the sale of pigs, Uncle George was my adviser. As with the cattle, we'd inspected them earlier. 'There', Uncle George had said, leaning over the wall of a sty and pointing at a large in-farrow sow, 'Her's a likely 'un. I should buy her if you can.' Other sows were rejected for varying reasons, but the one in the end sty met with his approval. 'Her's a fust class sow. Soak me bob, if her ain't. Her looks promising and not long to go by the looks on her.' Uncle opened the door and walked into the sty. The sow grunted and snuffled round his boots and Uncle scratched her back. 'Whoa, whoa, whoo, you're a nice quiet old thing, ain't you, my sweetheart? Whoo, whoo, whoo, I like the look of you.'

Uncle laid his hand holding the stick gently on the sow's back and bent over to count her teats. After a few moments he straightened up—the bending had made him very red in the face and a little breathless. 'Her've got sixteen dills, and by the looks of her, her'll need most of them afore long.'

I was able to buy both the sows selected by Uncle. And there was another sow, one that had been a favourite of Molly's; Mr Clutterbuck had given her to us. He would keep the sows and the cattle at Willow Farm until we moved to Perrygrove.

I bought a few implements, some tools and other equipment, all of which were laid out in rows in a meadow near the farmyard. Mr Bishop moved along the rows surrounded by the crowd, stopping at each item. 'How much am I bid, how much am I bid?' he chanted, putting in a quip or exhortation when bidding lagged. Once again Mr Saggamore was my adviser, though Uncle George accompanied us putting in a word or two of advice, sometimes sharply rebuked by Mr Saggamore. Not that a rebuff or two upset him, it took more than rebuffs to disconcert Uncle George. Except for an occasional 'have it your own way then', you'd never have thought he'd heard anything untoward. Uncle had had a few rebuffs in his time; but as he said often enough, 'you can't keep a good man down' especially when he doesn't know he's being rebuffed, as was usually the case with Uncle.

A lot of the stuff laid out in the meadow at Willow Farm found no eager buyers. Horse ploughs and the like, old farm wagons and carts, harness, a winnowing machine, butter churns, cheese presses, cream separators and other dairy equipment. So many machines with handles to turn, handles worn thin by human hands. Root pulpers, cattle-cake crushers—linseed, cotton and groundnut cake used to come in large, rectangular slabs—chaff machines, hay once being cut or chaffed, and a grindstone. Hardly anyone used them any more; those days of standing and turning and sweating were gone. Nobody wanted these hand powered machines; the work they did had also gone and they went cheaply for scrap. Years later they would be eagerly sought after and preserved, collectors items, but at this time it was merely out of date, useless junk, wanted by nobody.

The horse harness also went cheaply, though most of it was in good repair. Most farmers' harnesses were tattered, tied together with string; it was a sign of the times, few took much pride in the horse or its harness. The horses that remained spent most of their time idly in field or paddock while the tractor roared away at their former work, the horse only being used for odd jobs.

Jack and Bill stood watching the harness being sold.

'We could do with another set of short gears, aye us could,' said Bill. 'Why don't 'im buy them there?'

'I don't reckon the boss'll buy any more harness, and when our old mare do go, that'll be the last we shall see of 'osses at our place,' replied Jack.

'They'll 'ave ter bring 'osses back one day, aye 'em 'ull,' said Bill. 'It stands to reason.'

'I can't see it meself,' said Jack. 'I d'aim as they've 'ad ther day.'

Spades, shovels, pitchforks, hedge slashers, bill hooks, all things with handles. 'The only handles the young chaps know how to catch hold of be starting handles,' observed Jack, with the trace of a sneer, 'and most on 'em don't like them now, 'tis getting all self-starters—remember how us had to turn and turn that furst old tractor we ever had? And sometimes when 'er 'ad it on 'er, you could turn yer 'eart out.'

Mr Wrenn farmed next to Perrygrove. A solid, stocky squarely built man with a kindly rose-coloured face, probably in his mid-fifties. 'How-do, neighbour,' he said, puffing at his pipe, eyes twinkling. His hand shot out and he clasped mine. 'Any time you need help, you know where I live,' and off he stumped, trailing tobacco smoke behind him.

Molly was in the farmhouse helping Mrs Clutterbuck and her sister to prepare refreshments for Mr Bishop and his company, and for Mr Clutterbuck and his friends returning after the sale. I'd caught sight of them once or twice in the doorway of the kitchen, standing on tiptoe, craning their necks to see how far the sale had progressed.

Mr Bishop drew nearer to the sale of furniture—he was at present selling the odds and ends, chains, ropes, broken tools and heaps of stuff that were mainly rubbish. Mr Saggamore had lost all interest in the sale and was standing away, talking to friends. Uncle George was engaged in some blustering argument with a young man I didn't know; an interested circle of spectators had gathered round them and as I turned away I heard Uncle George call his adversary 'a bloody nogman'.

As I walked towards the house in search of Molly, Owen Tishforth, the haulier, caught me by the arm and said, 'They laughed about old Clutterbuck's cows, but today 'ave shown 'em.'

When Mr Bishop was auctioning the furniture, Molly became my mentor. We bought an aged oak dresser, it cost rather more than we could afford. As the bids got higher I stopped. Molly nudged me and said, 'Go on.' 'Done!' said Mr Bishop as I waved my catalogue.

But we bought the other furniture cheaply enough; plain but solid wooden chairs, pine cupboards, chest of drawers, dresser and table. Such furniture was too large for a number of the houses and farmers' wives no longer wanted furniture like it, although it would have been ideal for many farmhouses. They were disposing of furniture like this and replacing it with shining new mass produced stuff. Molly and I were left in no doubt that we were hopelessly behind the times; and we were. But as it turned out, in front of them too.

And so we prepared to go to Perrygrove Farm. With little money, but plenty of ideas, hopes and enthusiasm. Little did we realise that our way of life would soon become as old fashioned as the furniture we'd just bought.

CHAPTER SEVEN

Moving in

Perrygrove Farm, with eighty-five acres of level fertile land, was known locally as a useful little place. Pastures, plough-land and orchards; small fields sheltered by hedges and trees, elm, oak and ash. Alder and willow trees grew on the banks of the stream that ran through some of the fields. The barns, loose boxes, pig sties, the stable with hayloft, the cowshed with the low slate roof patterned by green and gold lichen, and the other buildings were conveniently grouped around the farmyard. An important point this, as so much time was spent, especially during winter months, going from one building to another.

The rectangular seventeenth century farmhouse of

77

mellowed brick was large, far too large for just Molly and me. The garden was neglected; the lawns and borders unkempt, no trees or shrubs; the vegetable garden undug and full of weeds, docks, thistles, nettles, brambles and ranging raspberries gone wild. 'Good farmers are bad gardeners', was a current saying. And it was true that not many farmers liked gardening. Even Mr Saggamore who hated to see a square yard of land idle was a reluctant gardener. Until late in April the vegetable garden at Suttridge was a sorry state with sprout stems waving in the wind, decaying cabbages, and parsnips with bold new growth of leaves. He was inordinately fond of parsnips and planted even more than he could eat—or, what was more likely, more than Mrs Saggamore would cook. And then one day at the end of April, invariably a market day, Mr Saggamore would order everyone into the garden.

Grabbing a spade he would set-to with a will, plunging the spade into the earth, blade flashing as he turned the soil over and thrust it into the upturned earth. 'Turns over a treat now,' he'd say. 'Mistake to get on the garden too early, when it's wet and unkind, but, by jove, it's just right today, nice and friable.'

When he had us all busy, digging, wheeling away cabbage stumps and returning with barrow loads of short manure, he would suddenly stop and look at his watch. 'By jove, time's gone on, I must go and get ready for market.'

Like most farmers of his age, he rarely missed going to market; it was their day out when they met friends and business acquaintances. Once their business was done in the market—if they had any, and often they hadn't but they pretended they had; and of course business didn't just mean selling or buying at the auction—they went to one of the numerous public houses around the market. Each farmer and each salesman had his favourite pub and people knew they could be found there. The new men and the younger men coming into farming rarely visited the pubs and if they did they didn't linger there long. The market pubs were open all day long and the older farmers took full advantage of it.

Before leaving for market he would visit us again, in checked jacket, widely cut breeches and box-cloth leggings; newly shaved and smelling strongly of soap. 'That's right, lads. Set-to with a will and you'll soon have it done. I only wish I could stop and give you a hand, but I've got to get to market. There's a man I must see most partic'lar, about a bit of business. I must go, it's most important. You'll have it all done by the time I get back.'

'If 'im's so fond on't, why do 'im allus choose a market day for't?' Bill would say as Mr Saggamore drove off.

On the morning of 30th September, the day after Michaelmas Day, Molly and I were standing in front of the house at Perrygrove waiting for Owen Tishforth to arrive with our chattels. Owen was late as he so frequently was. 'Where is he?' asked Molly, impatient to begin. 'He should have been here twenty minutes ago. Mrs Gymble will be here soon.' Mrs Gymble lived in a cottage about half a mile away and she was coming to help Molly with the house, the furniture, carpets and curtains.

Between looking anxiously down the road and listening for the sound of Owen's lorry, Molly made plans for the garden. 'We'll have a lilac in that corner,' she said, pointing, 'and some hollyhocks under the wall.'

We'd helped Owen load and he'd said he had to go back to his home first before coming over to Perrygrove.

'I can't understand what's delayed him,' said Molly. I knew Owen well enough to know that it didn't take much to delay him. Although Molly had been in the district some years now she still couldn't quite understand, or get accustomed to some of our people and their little ways.

'We could train a rose to grow over that porch—and there's room there for a wistaria. Oh, where is Owen?'

79

'Perhaps his lorry's broken down.'

'That's what Mr Clutterbuck used to say when he was waiting for Owen to take something to market. I'm sure a lot of the animals would have made more money if Owen had got them to market on time. You're all too soft with that man, making excuses for him.'

'His lorry is getting very old.'

'Why doesn't he buy a new one?'

It would have been difficult for him to muster the money without doing his books and sending out accounts. Owen was an agreeable fellow, willing to do most things, but there was one thing he wouldn't do and that was accounts. It seemed he would rather go without the money than do them.

Uncle George arrived.

'Well, damn my rags,' he exclaimed when he'd finished huffing and puffing and squeezing himself out of his van. 'Ain't this yer garden in a bloody mommuck. J'know, I never realised when I was here afore as it was so wild, 'cos I never stopped just here, I went on round yonder there. Tidy enough round the buildings I remember thinking to meself—but 'pon my soul, he've let it go here, 'aven't he? Right by the road as you might say. Here, I think I'd better go round to the vegetable garden an' see what sort of a state 'e've got it in there.'

We followed a muttering Uncle George round to the vegetable garden. He surveyed the desolation there in silence for a while. He shook his head in disgust. At last he spoke.

'Never had much off 'ere this year, nor last by the look on't. 'Aven't put a spade in 'ere for some time.' Uncle George wrinkled his nose and pouted with distaste. He kicked the toe of his boot into the undug ground. 'Good ground, too. Wants some rotted pig manure on 'ere an' a damn good deep digging. Well, well, well, damn my rags, I'm surprised Barnard let it go like this. Not a currant bush, not even a clump o' rhubarb. Nothing but them raspberries gone wild, look at 'em everywhere.' He slashed at some raspberry canes with his stick. 'Allus thought he were an up together fella. Good farmer too. Oh, I know farmers ain't the best of chaps in a garden.' Uncle spoke very slowly, looking very solemn and wise, an exercise that necessitated a lot of cheek blowing, nose wrinkling, eye widening, and the dropping of his voice several tones. 'But most on 'em ain't quite as bad as this.' A long pause. 'But I don't know', he rumbled, 'I s'pose some on 'em be. Some on 'em today don't like a bit of hard graft in the garden. Got their backsides cocked on a tractor, that's more to their liking today.' Uncle pondered in gloomy silence. Molly and I knew him too well in this mood to interrupt. Suddenly he cocked his head up and said decisively, 'We'll have to odds it.'

'I shan't have time, not yet. I must get the ground ploughed and planted,' I said quickly, before Molly could speak.

'Yes, yes,' rumbled Uncle, 'of course you will. Don't you worry about it, you've got plenty to do without the bother of this. I'll arrange for old Colonel to come over and make a start on't. Old Colonel's a fairish hand in the garden. That is, mind you, if he's supervised.' Uncle looked very knowingly. 'I'll come over and tutor him a bit. The screws is playing me up a bit, but I'll be able to keep an eye on him.'

By this time we'd walked back round to the front. 'I wonder where Owen is?' said Molly.

'I can tell you where he was', said Uncle George, 'He was at The Lion when I came by, 'cos I saw his lorry outside.'

'Well, I hope he'll hurry up,' said Molly.

'He should be here directly, 'cos when I saw his lorry outside I nipped into The Lion and gave him a piece of my mind. I said to him, I said, "them two young people'll be hangin' about waitin' for you, Owen," I said. An' he said,— 'cos I spoke to him sharply mind,—"Old 'ard, Jarge," 'e said, "I bin 'ard at it all marnin'". "Ard at it, be buggered", I said,

81

"you be squat 'ere swillin' beer when you oughter be on yer way." "I'm 'avin me bait" 'e said, pullin' at a great hunk of bread and cheese. "I ain't 'ad anythin' all marnin'." "Well, for God's sake yut up an' drink up an' get a move on," I told'n. O' course, I can see now, I oughter've stopped there with'n and seen as the varmint made a move sharpish, but I was anxious to get on over 'ere.'

'We can't do a thing until he comes,' I said.

'He's messing up the whole day,' complained Molly.

'I can't understand the feller,' said Uncle George. 'Allus was the same. Allus late. Nice enough fella, but allus the same. Can't pass a pub when it's open, that's the trouble. The hours he's hindered me. Dilatory, dilatory. The times I've kicked my heels up of a mornin' waitin' for the varmint to come and pick my pigs up for market—and the pubs ain't even open at that time. The times I've been goin' to cuss him up hill and down dale. But I never have, 'cos when he do come, he's so nice and obliging and friendly, I haven't had the heart to. Still, he oughter be here by now, it's too bad of the fellow.'

'I'll give him a piece of my mind when he does come,' said Molly.

'No, no, you won't, my dear,' said Uncle. ''Cos when he comes, he'll be so nice and smiling and helpful that your heart'll soften. You'll make him a cup o' tea instead, and fuss over him. Everybody does.' He gave a rumbling chuckle that went on and on and seemed to end up gurgling in his boots.

'I want a lilac bush over there in that corner,' said Molly.

'Laylack,' said Uncle, 'my mother loved laylack. You've sin that gurt laylack down at my place? My father planted that for her the year before he died. Yes, a laylack 'ould look very nice over in that corner. That 'ould've pleased my dear mother, to see a laylack over there. You'd have got on well with mother, my dear. She was very fond of flowers, my mother was. Christmas roses was another of her favourites, and hollyhocks and sweet williams.'

'I thought about planting hollyhocks under the wall,' said Molly.

'We must make a start as soon as possible,' said Uncle George, 'I'll bring Old Colonel over and put him in the way of things as soon as I've a day to spare. And if my back's playin' me up, I can allus sit on a box and keep an eye on him—and that reminds me, I've got a little cask of cider in the van.' Uncle gave me a knowing wink. 'You can always get a bit of help when you want it if chaps know you've got a drop of cider about the place. Owen can give me a hand with it when he gets here.'

Mrs Gymble swung into the yard on her bicycle, one of those old-fashioned bicycles with a dressguard over the rear wheel. She dismounted nimbly, despite her size; she was large and plump. The bicycle was discarded the moment it had served its purpose, and was flung clattering against a wall.

'Where's Owen Tishforth?' she demanded, 'Where is he?' Her fresh complexioned face looked at us accusingly, as though we were responsible for Owen's absence. Any minute I expected her to ask what we'd done with him, where we'd put him. Instead, she said briskly, 'Well, come on. It's no good standing here, let's go inside and see what we can do. But I'll let Tishforth have it hot and strong when he does get here, the tow-rag. He'll learn it don't do to keep Alice Gymble waiting.'

'Hark! Hark!' Uncle stood rigid and cupped a hand to his ear. 'I think I can hear him a comin'. That's his old lorry I can hear. Yes, yes, here he is, turning up here. Mind, he's a hardworkin' chap, about with that old lorry of his at all hours of the day and night, wikdays and Sundays. Very obliging and affable, allus comes, even if he is a bit late. You can't begrudge the poor old devil a drink.'

Owen drew up alongside us and poked his bristly,

grinning face out of the window. 'Thought I'd find you here,' he said, and grinned wider than ever, exposing his gappy mouth.

'You've got here then, Owen,' said Uncle George, as if Owen had travelled a thousand miles.

'Good-morning, Mr Tishforth,' said Molly, smiling at him.

'Nice morning for the time of year, ain't it?' said Owen cheerfully. He put a cigarette in his mouth, lit it and with an arm leaning on the door, he sat back, blew smoke out through the window, grinned, scratched his chin, tugged at the lobe of his ear, and between all these activities muttered, 'Oh ah, oh ah,' until Mrs Gymble came bounding round the corner.

'Come on, Tishforth! Back that lorry up here by the door. Don't just sit there grinning like a half-witted codfish! You've wasted enough time already, you varmint!'

'Oh ah, oh ah,' said Owen pleasantly, 'Right-ho.'

'And look sharp about it, or you'll have me to reckon with,' shouted Mrs Gymble.

Once the tail board of the lorry was lowered, Mrs Gymble seized a sweeping broom and looked almost warlike, a spark of battle gleaming in her eye. From that moment on her presence was like that of a whirlwind. She bullied Uncle George, Owen and me as we carried the furniture. When Uncle complained about its weight she caught hold of it herself, pushing and heaving through doorways and exclaiming, 'Men, men, they're all the same, all moans and groans when it comes to work.' She rattled buckets and pans, wielded a sweeping broom with unnecessary force and vigour. She unrolled and laid the carpets with aplomb. Actually, carpets is a rather grandiose term for what amounted to one small carpet (secondhand and past its best) and several lengths of coconut matting. 'Have linoleum, it's so serviceable,' Molly had been advised, but she had an aversion to linoleum and chose the matting—which, by and by, she came to hate. Coconut matting, as Molly was to discover, attracted dust and dirt with magnetic and infuriating power.

Mrs Gymble pumped water, splashed water, and busied herself generally in ways that were wonderful if rather frightening to behold. She shouted and roared at us—Molly was the only one who was immune; somehow she regarded Molly as her sole ally in what I was beginning to think was her private battle against the universe. Even Uncle George was intimidated by her vigour and apparent ferocity. But it was Owen who was the main recipient of her chastisement, and yet Owen was the least perturbed. Owen could never believe that anyone could be angry with him, not really angry. 'Steady on, missus,' he cajoled, 'Get on with your work, Owen Tishforth,' she ordered, 'and don't you "missus" me. I'm not your missus, if I had've been you'd have been a different man to-day. I'd 've put a stop to some of your little ways.'

'Now, now, don't take on so,' murmured Owen.

'Don't just stand there muttering. Be about your work,' retorted Mrs Gymble, and rattled the broom about Owen's feet. 'And make sure you have some coal here by ten o'clock tomorrow, or you'll have me to reckon with,' she warned Owen before she left.

'Phew!' said Uncle George when she'd departed and peace had returned to Perrygrove, 'I couldn't do with a performance like that very often.'

Later, Owen brought the cows from Willow Farm, 'Better put 'em in the cowshed and let 'em settle down', said Uncle George. 'The ones that need milking 'll be ready for you then.'

To drive four cows into an empty shed and tie them up is easily done—or so I thought. The cows at Suttridge walked into their shed, each standing patiently in her place, waiting for the chain to be fastened round her neck. But these four cows wouldn't be coaxed or driven into the shed. 'Strange shed, strange people, strange cows, all strange and no cow as knows 'er way to lead 'em,' said Owen. The cows would get within a yard or two of the door, our hopes would rise. 'Gently, gently, don't rush 'em,' whispered Owen. One would actually put her nose round the doorway and sniff and then quickly turn and rush away, taking the others with her. Uncle George huffed and puffed, 'Rajah rhubarb!' he said, 'It's a buggeroo, damn my rags if it ain't.'

Success looked imminent when all four again approached the doorway, heads down, sniffing suspiciously, but with legs cautiously moving in the right direction. Owen, Uncle and I, arms outstretched, followed them at a discreet distance. Suddenly they wheeled round and with lowered heads charged past us and then stood sulkily and unmovingly in a tight group in the yard. We tried enticing them with hay and then with some cubes of cattle cake, laying a trail of it into the cowshed. But to no avail. 'If we could just get 'em inside we could shut the blasted door on 'em a bit bloody quick,' said Uncle George. But now they wouldn't go near the door; they hung about in a corner of the yard looking distressed and perplexed. 'Get your missus to give a hand,' suggested Owen, adding hopefully, 'They do know her, may be they'll go in for her.' Molly came, but if the cows recognised her they failed to show it. I began to wish the forceful Mrs Gymble was still with us; surely no cow could possibly defy her? 'I'm fair bathered,' said Uncle George, mopping his head with a big spotted handkerchief.

'I'll make a pot of tea,' said Molly.

'Ah, now that's a good idea,' said Owen, 'give 'em a chance to find their bearings.'

After we'd had the tea, we went back out and found the cows all meekly standing in the shed. 'Shut the door quick, afore they change their minds,' said Uncle.

CHAPTER EIGHT

Early Days

My first and most pressing task was ploughing. The stubbles had to be ploughed and cultivated ready for the sowing of autumn corn. Ideally, the corn should be planted during the third week in October. If planted earlier it would 'get away too quickly', 'become too forward', as we said, meaning the growth would be too much and while it would look good at Christmas, later it would suffer. Instead of a thick, lush growth, it was far better to have a plant that just clung to the ground with sparse growth, then it would stand the winter. But not too sparse a growth. The corn needed planting early enough for it to get established and build up a good root system before the hard weather came.

And there was another equally pressing reason for planting early; the danger of the ground becoming too wet,
making cultivations and drilling difficult. 'Sow wheat in
slop', was part of an old saying, and though better to drill in
friable ground it was true that wheat could thrive when
planted in such conditions. But on our land with its heavy
clay subsoil, prolonged rain soon made it impossible for the
passage of tractors. The wheels would spin, sending up a
shower of mud, and as the wheels churned the soggy ground
they slowly sank lower and lower until the tractor could
move neither forwards nor backwards. Of course, this is
where horses had the advantage over them; you could still
get on land with horses when it was impossible with tractors.
But there was a better chance of getting the work finished
with tractors while conditions were still reasonable. I cannot
stress this point too strongly; tractors and other machinery
had a much better opportunity of beating the weather.

I spent the first few weeks ploughing with my little grey
tractor, the white billowing clouds and the white, squawking, greedy seagulls for company. Pigs are greedy and
quarrelsome when feeding, but I think seagulls are greedier
and more quarrelsome when feeding on worms behind the
plough. Ploughing is a satisfying occupation, the best ever
devised by man; ploughing more than almost any other
farmwork comes closer to the townsman's conception of
rural tranquillity. "The ploughman homeward plods his
weary way", after plodding behind and handling a plough all
day. But not any more; the tractor has taken the physical
labour out of ploughing. The touch of a knob and my
two-furrow plough lifts out of the ground when I reach the
headland, and I turn the tractor with my other hand as easily
as turning a motor car; another touch of the knob and the
plough is lowered and I'm off down the field again, followed
by the raucous seagulls.

Very different from the cumbersome old tractors and

trailing ploughs we had only a few years earlier. To lift and lower the plough then, we had to tug on a lever; sometimes the plough failed to lift, the tractor required the force of both arms to turn it at the headlands. Occasionally, we found ourselves battling with plough and tractor and surging crabwise into the ditch.

Ploughing by tractor meant, of course, a constant turning of the head to see the plough. With horse ploughing the plough was right in front of your eyes; it did make for a closer affinity with the soil and undoubtedly for greater care and pride in ploughing. But this was true of all horse work. Now with the quickening tempo, the standards of pride and care in farmwork began to slip.

As soon as the ploughing was done, I put the cultivator first across, and then up and down the furrows, stirring the earth and breaking up the clods. Mr Saggamore stood watching, nodding his approval; for Mr Saggamore loved the heavy cultivator above all tillage implements. I stopped the tractor and, dismounting spoke to him. The toe of his boot scuffed through the loose mould. 'This ground'll grow wheat,' he said, meaning that it was good wheat land. 'Don't get too fine a tilth or it'll run together and set like concrete,' he advised. 'Give it a couple of hundredweights to the acre of compound and you should get a good crop.' I saw his brow wrinkle and watched his lips moving silently. I knew him so well that I guessed he was estimating how many tons of corn the field should yield, and at so much per ton the probable value of the crop. Sure enough, his brow cleared; 'It should bring a tidy little cheque,' he said.

The auctioneers, Mr Bishop and Mr Rolls, each with an assistant came to do the valuation. The quantity of hay and straw was estimated, a number of bales were weighed on a spring balance and calculations were made. Hay bales were cut open, the hay was examined, handled, sniffed. Mr Rolls commented favourably on the quality; Mr Bishop was noncommittal. Both made entries in their notebooks. Hedges, fences, ditches, ponds were scrutinised and so were the fields. Later invoices from The Farmers' Stores were produced showing the quantities of fertilisers and animal foods used in recent years, from which the auctioneers would calculate the value of the unexhausted manurial residues. Mr Bishop's object would be to keep the valuation down as low as possible. Mr Rolls, acting for Mr Barnard, would endeavour to get as high a valuation as possible. If both Barnard and I were equally dissatisfied, it would prove that the outcome of their deliberations had been fair and just. It wasn't, as you may suppose, conducted in a strained atmosphere. On the contrary, the day passed very pleasantly. As we walked the farm, the auctioneers strode ahead conversing amicably about their business, recent happenings, and the prospects of the season's foxhunting. The two assistants, young men apprenticed to the auctioneers, walked side by side and discussed rugby football. Barnard and I lagged behind; every so often he stopped and pointed out something to me and made various observations such as 'that's a funny old bit of ground', or 'it always lies a bit wet over there', which would be of use to me in the future.

I borrowed a corn drill. Colonel rode on the back to see the seed flowed down the spouts and into the ground. We drilled the headland, six times round the field. As was always the case with the headlands we seemed to use an inordinate amount of seed; a quarter of it gone and we'd not really started. The wheat was Cappelle, a new high yielding variety. We started drilling up and down the field; Colonel had to lift the coulters out of the ground when we reached the headland, and lower them when we'd turned and started the return journey. Every so often we had to stop and tip more seed into the hopper. As we neared the end of the field, the usual question: should we have enough seed to finish? The drilling was completed—with half a bag of corn to spare—and the corn was harrowed in.

I went to the market with Mr Saggamore and bought two cows. As we stood looking at them afterwards the vendor came and pressed a ten shilling note into my hand. 'Luck money', he explained. An acquaintance of Mr Saggamore's, pointing to one of the cows, said 'She's got a divided bag.' 'No matter', replied Mr Saggamore, sharply, 'the milk'll be same price, divided bag or not.'

All around us the hustle of market day; cattle bellowing, pigs squealing, sheep bleating, lorries roaring, handbells ringing; and auctioneers, farmers, dealers, drovers, shouting, talking, laughing. Farmers and others thronged into the market. They stood about in groups gossiping or jostled round the pens of animals being sold. Tall men, short men, fat ones, thin ones. Burly men, not unlike the fat animals being sold, and wizened up little men. Men with weather-beaten faces, big red faces, open honest faces, cunning faces. Some dressed in bright checked jackets, breeches and leggings, others in blue serge suits. Some in white riding macs, others in grubby raincoats. Well dressed or shabby, their apparel was no guide to their prosperity, though even the most smartly dressed farmers were unable to rival the sartorial splendour of Mr Bishop, in his grey bowler hat and yellow waistcoat, as he stood high above them while he auctioned the several pens of sheep.

Wooden huts of the various merchants, the seed and corn merchants, the fertiliser merchants, lime, hay and straw merchants, cattle food and machinery merchants. The salesmen who brought and displayed their wares, harness, ropes, halters, rabbit snares, calf muzzles, cattle medicines, pig troughs, hay racks for sheep and cattle. Constant exhortations from the down-at-heel looking drovers to 'mind your backs there', or 'turn 'em in there', as they penned, loaded, or unloaded animals from the grunting lorries.

In one corner of the market, quieter than elsewhere and close to the high brick wall, stood a refreshment stall, rather like the London coffee stalls in appearance, where a few men would stand and drink strong tea out of thick earthenware cups and hold roughly cut sandwiches which they would push into their mouths. But most farmers preferred to find refreshment in one of the dozen public houses which surrounded the market. The pubs did a roaring trade, farmers and beer spilled out on to the streets. The shops also did well—for the farmer despite his alleged meanness spent freely on market days.

After I'd been to the auctioneer's office to pay for the cows, we found Owen Tishforth and arranged for him to transport the cows to Perrygrove. Then Mr Saggamore took me to his favourite public house, into a small back room crowded with his friends, most of whom I already knew.

Mr Troy, whose company sold agricultural machinery, a tall, bespectacled man, with wide shoulders, his body tapering down to small feet, seeing us enter, cried, 'What'll you have?'

Hesketh Newman, an old friend of Saggamore's, was standing by the bar, talking and smoking a cigarette, dropping ash on his waistcoat. As always, he was wearing a bowler hat, bow tie and a long, hunting style jacket. A well known and popular man, now in his seventies, he combined farming with cattle dealing, wrote for various newspapers and still hunted twice a week during the season.

Hugh Corrigan was there in an old torn jacket—'got pots of money', Mr Saggamore once told me—asking little Mr Moore, one of the county's leading farmers, to lend him a pound to buy a round of drinks. Slumped in a chair in the corner was Roger Warren, an arable farmer, with a surly expression on his face which belied his generous nature. Warren was a heavy drinker, a devil-may-care man who'd do anything for a dare; ready to fight anybody who'd take him on—and, on occasion, some who weren't. On horseback he'd jump the widest ditch, the highest hedge. Edward Richardson was talking to Harry Hooker. Richardson took most of the prizes at the Christmas Fatstock Show. Hooker, it was said, 'couldn't keep his hands off women'. Roger Warren took an interest in Hooker's amorous exploits, and was always predicting, apropos of some woman or other, that, 'there'd soon be another little Hooker about'.

The small room was thick with tobacco smoke and loud with talk. The men who gathered here every market day had turned the place into a kind of club, to which only a select few could belong. I never discovered the qualifications, but, because of Mr Saggamore, I was allowed to join. I knew that it would be late afternoon before the last of them staggered out and even back in the market they would stand about in a little group, still talking.

Several of the salesmen in that fuggy little room wanted to buy me a drink. I was a farmer now and a potential customer. Even when walking through the market with Mr Saggamore I was hailed by salesmen now.

Agreeable though it was, I soon left the company. I was anxious to return to Perrygrove before Owen delivered the cows. Mr Saggamore remained. I'd met Mr Wrenn in the market and he'd promised me a ride home. Just as I was leaving, however, Mr Newman came and spoke to me and followed me to the doorway, 'And when you employ labour,' he said, putting his hand on my shoulder, 'don't forget they've got to stick at it all day. A farmer's his own master, he can stop, go to the house and have a cigarette, do something else, but a farmworker has to stick at it. I've seen so many farmers go into the barn, or the field, and work like hell for a quarter of an hour, showing their men up and saying that's the way to do it. But they forget they don't have to stick at it.'

Back at Perrygrove, I'd fed the pigs, milked the cows and had my tea and still Owen hadn't brought the cows from market. Dusk was falling before he arrived, 'Where have you been?' I asked. 'Got delayed,' replied Owen, in his matter of fact way. He lowered the tailboard of his lorry and said, 'No need to worry. I've got 'em here safe and sound.' Owen was a skilled practitioner; a soothing word and disarming smile.

Luckily the cows went into the shed without any difficulty. Milk was squirting from their swollen udders—it was the practice not to milk them on the morning of their sale. I felt annoyed with Owen, I would have milked them in the market to ease them had I known, but Owen had promised to have them at Perrygrove within two hours. I got a bucket and stool and sat down to milk. Owen stood in the cowshed and talked as I did so; and before I'd finished the second cow I began to think that Owen wasn't such a bad fellow after all.

Next day, while waiting for the Ministry Vet, I started to dig the vegetable garden. The state of the garden had been nagging at me. Molly had already forked over a flower border and the sight of it served as a reproof to me. I'd had a letter from the Ministry Vet telling me that he'd be calling about my attested licence. When I heard the slam of a car door I guessed it announced the Vet's arrival; I thrust the spade into the earth and went to meet him.

A tall big boned man stepped out of the car, gave me a firm handclasp and in a thick Scottish accent wished me

'Good afternoon.' We went into the kitchen and after sitting down he pulled out a sheaf of papers from a case and placed them on the table. His accent was so thick that apart from a word here and there, he might as well have been conversing in a foreign language. 'I'm sorry', I said at the beginning, 'I didn't quite ...' But the time soon came when I just couldn't ask him to repeat himself again and again. I clung to the few words I recognised and tried to weave sentences round them. That unfamiliar voice continued, accompanied from time to time by a rustle of papers as he flicked through them. I answered, 'Yes', or 'no', and I nodded or shook my head in what I could only hope were the correct places. And then, seeing my blank stare and receiving no answer, he repeated the same list of sounds; among them I identified the word 'fences'. 'Yes', I answered, 'there's a double fence all round the farm.' (The regulations require a double fence round the perimeter of an attested farm). 'Good', he said, and what followed was incomprehensible. He bent over and fished a form out from the case at his feet. I had a choice of whether my attested premium should be paid on the amount of milk I sold, or a yearly payment on the number of cattle. I chose payment on the milk—or that's what I hoped I'd done.

The Vet had only just left when another car arrived. I guessed immediately, by the false bonhommie and the effusive smile, that the man who stepped out of the car, was here to try and sell me something. I'd learnt already, in the few weeks I'd been at Perrygrove, that part of the art of farming was resisting buying stuff you didn't need in the face of salesmen determined to sell their products. Being a new farmer, the word must have gone round fairly quickly in the commercial travellers' world and I was plagued by them. They descended on Perrygrove like pigeons on laid corn. Oil salesmen were the most numerous and their persistence was only equalled by the cattle medicine salesmen. The food merchants, machinery merchants, fertiliser salesmen, lime men, men selling dairy detergents and insurance men, while lacking nothing in persuasion or persistence, did not stay for so long; compared to the oil and medicine men they were easy to get rid of—though if only to return again in a few weeks time. But the oil men who only visited a district a few times in a year stuck their ground. The medicine man's itinerary took him only once or twice a year to the same farm. They could afford and indeed did spend half a day trying to get an order. The art which I was painfully learning wasn't only to resist their glib patter, but also to prevent them from wasting too much of my time. They pressed samples on me, charts, catalogues, brochures, leaflets, order forms, pens and pencils.

This man, with confident tread and outstretched hand, was a medicine man. I had become quite adept at guessing correctly what their line of business was, even before they spoke. However, before I'd even realised it, this man was vigorously shaking my hand and addressing me by name. I rather resented this name business, he'd looked it up in his book or asked at the previous farm—they all did it.

'I represent WARNE AND SPICER, Tinkerpoof's the name. In the war, injured, wife left me. All right now, married again. Of course you've heard of me; old established firm, manufacturers of cattle medicines, remedies, minerals, sundries, valuable aids to livestock farmers, appliances. High repute, suppliers to most of the leading breeders in this country and abroad; highly recommended by all stockmen, our stands at all the major shows up and down the country, successful exhibitors ...' All this non stop. But now he took a breath, through his mouth in mid-sentence, and continued with increased vigour, '... all use our cattle shampoos, some say half the pedigree goes in at the mouth, but the rosette it is truly said by others, successful men, and they should know, the rosettes go on with Warne and Spicers shampoo. Cattle men the world over,' (he sucked in air greedily), 'swear by

Warne and Spicer's remedies. Nobody else can touch 'em. Now, there's several things you'll be needing.'

He rushed back to his car and returned with a handful of leaflets and thrust them into my hands.

'Just a few of our products, brief descriptions, directions, symptoms, handy containers, always advisable to buy the larger sizes, more economical', (another intake of breath, his face getting redder), 'only call once a year, large area to cover, you'll remember my name, Tinkerpoof, only one in the book, ring any time, quick service, all goods despatched on the day of ordering. Any trouble, don't hesitate to get in touch with me. Always reach me by telephone before nine in the morning', (more air), 'and after six at night, weekdays or Sundays, always at the farmers' service, here's my card, no, have two in case you lose one, doesn't matter really, can't forget my name, the only one in the book, farmers always ringing me for advice. Just a minute.'

He went to his car and brought back several small tins and bottles which he placed on the wall beside me. 'Just a few samples,—no charge,—absolutely free, you'll find them useful, very effective. Just a moment while I get my order book.'

Notebook in hand, he took a deep breath and was about to continue.

'But,' I said, 'I don't—' He held up his hand and started speaking before I could finish.

'Worms, farmers don't realise the toll worms take, profits slipping away, unthrifty cattle all because of worms, lower milk yields, calves not thriving', (a deep intake of breath, mouth open, saliva forming on his lips, because he couldn't pause to swallow), 'pigs not fattening, sheep coughing, all because of worms; we have worming preparations for all classes of cattle, sheep, pigs, poultry; you have cattle of course, cattle, milking cows and calves.'

'Yes, but ...'

'Sheep? Any sheep?'

'No, but ...'

'No sheep. But you've pigs, pigs very susceptible to worms, and you'll need minerals, powder form for pigs; have general purpose unless you have any specific trouble, cattle minerals in blocks, powder blocks, advise powder, more economical, have to use so much salt to make the blocks, have powder.'

'I don't really need ...'

'No specific problems', (writing in notebook), 'have general purpose, shall we say five hundredweight, discount on five hundredweight or over, prices include', (breath, face very red, little veins standing out on his forehead), 'carriage paid to your door like all our products. Anything urgent sent by post; otherwise—although, I've been known to deliver myself, keep an extensive range at home for emergencies, all part', (breath), 'of my service to farmers, built up my business on service and goodwill. Chills, winter coming on, stock bound to get chills, especially calves, our *CHILLAWAY* very effective, six drenches to a bottle, cases of one or two dozen, cheaper to have the larger size, two dozen case, never know you want it until you need it. Scouring,—scouring can be a problem, our *SCOURGO* tablets are second to none, box of fifty, always ring me if you want more. After calving pick-me-up, I can', (breath), 'recommend our *AFTERCALFO*. Bloat, not much of a problem now perhaps, but you never know ...'

'I'm afraid I'm rather busy, and ...'

'I know, I know, won't keep you a minute, being as quick as I can. Bloat, in the spring, won't be around for twelve months, our *BURPO* has saved many a beast. Cows not coming into season, can't beat our *HISEXY*, packets of six. Udder cream, salve, ointment for sores. Calving drenches', (a deep throaty breath, eyes dilating), 'drenches for retained afterbirths, *MOTHERMOO* and *RIDOFIT*, are sovereign remedies. Our *DANDY* is a wonderful tonic, cow off her food, anything like that, *DANDY's* the stuff for her, never fails with listless animals.'

He continued like this for some time, and I stood there, bemused and unable to complete a sentence. From his car he extracted more leaflets, booklets and samples which he passed on to me. From his top pocket he produced two pencils, embossed with WARNE AND SPICER in gilt. And just before he left he presented me with a calving chart and notebook, both embossed WARNE AND SPICER: The Friend of the Farmer and his Livestock.

'I mustn't hinder you. I can see you're a busy man like me. Pleasure to meet you. Any time, any time.'

I ordered some minerals, worming mixture and half a dozen bottles of *DANDY* tonic. 'Thank you, thank you', he said, 'any time you're in trouble or need advice, remember me, only Tinkerpoof in the book. Any time you need anything, just telephone before nine or after six. Or if it's only to give an order you can telephone during the day, my wife is always there.'

'Who was that?' asked Molly, as I went indoors for a cup of coffee.

'Man selling cattle medicines. We've had some travellers, but he beats the lot. Never stopped talking. I couldn't get a word in edgeways. Still, I got rid of him in the end. I ordered a few minerals and worming drenches and half a dozen bottles of tonic.'

CHAPTER NINE

Fall of the Year

There was a sharp nip in the air. The roadside verges were still powdered with white frost as I rode my bicycle along the narrow road overshadowed by tall hedges. The tall hedges reminded me that now I'd planted the wheat, I should have to tackle the hedges at Perrygrove. I remembered a remark Mr Saggamore made, 'Once you let your hedges go ...'

I was going to see a Colonel Ashley. On Mr Bishop's instigation I'd written to him, and by return of post I received a postcard naming a date and time, and the brief sentence 'I have six cows for sale.' Molly had suggested that I borrow Uncle George's van. 'What?' I replied, 'it's only about three miles. There's no sense in cycling five miles to borrow a van to go three miles.'

'Very well,' she said, 'but I expect he lives in a grand place and it won't look very good, you arriving on a bike.'

'Huh!' I'd scoffed. But now arriving at the large Georgian house, set well back from the road and reached by means of an imposing driveway flanked by stately trees, I thought there was something in what she'd said. Uncle George's van wasn't much, but it would have been better than my rusty old bicycle. I dumped the thing, into the ditch under the roadside hedge, feeling a bit disloyal, and hoped the Colonel wouldn't notice it or ask how I'd come.

I walked up the drive—I was wearing my new breeches, stockings and heavy brown brogues—and past a large, well trimmed lawn, big as a cricket pitch. There were sedate flower beds with Michaelmas daisies, Japanese anemones, gaillardias and heleniums still flowering. Part of the house was covered by a climbing rose, its profusion of delicate pink bloom slightly damaged by the weather. The gravel crunched beneath my feet. I stopped and wiped my shoes on the mat and then stepped far enough inside the porch to pull the round ornate iron bell pull. I heard the bell jangling and echoing inside the house. As I waited I noticed several pairs of gumboots, walking sticks and umbrellas beside me in the porch. The door was opened by a middle-aged man, who was rather short and wore a jacket with leather patches on the elbows and leather binding round the cuffs, and baggy grey flannel trousers. His eyes blinked behind his spectacles as I told him who I was.

'Yes, I was expecting you,' he said, in a crisp but pleasant voice. 'Just a minute, while I put some boots on.' He bent down and untied his shoe laces, kicked off his shoes and pulled on a pair of gumboots. 'Right', he said, marching down the drive, 'it's not far, I think we'll walk. I'm overstocked and I think these cows might suit you.'

When we reached the end of the drive he stopped, and he peered up and down the road; sharply, first to the right and then to the left and then to the right again. He looked puzzled. 'How did you come?' he asked quickly, but not sharply. I hesitated, but his glance was now on the bicycle in the ditch. 'By bicycle,' I said.

'That's it there? That's your bicycle, is it?'

'Yes.'

He chuckled, and then smiling at me, he said, 'I've never had anyone come to buy cows on a bicycle before. I think that's very clever of you. Very clever indeed.'

'Clever?' I asked, perfectly at ease now.

'Yes, you thought you'd get the cows cheaper by coming on a bicycle, and you might, so you might. It appeals to me.'

We walked across a field. 'There', said Colonel Ashley, raising his walking stick and using it to point at a new asbestos-roofed shed, 'that's my milking shed. We'll go there first, my cowman will be there. It's a short cut through the field.' He shot a glance at my shoes, 'Not very suitable footwear to come buying cows in.' He prodded several cow pats with a stick, the pasture was thick with them. He stopped and prodded more in quick succession. 'They talk about heavy stocking', he said, 'but just look at this.'

The cowshed was big, with a double row of standings, a wide passage way down the middle. The concrete floor was wet and spotlessly clean; the tubular stalls, yokes and mangers were immaculate. 'We only had this put up last year,' said Colonel Ashley. 'Had the devil of a job getting the builder to hurry up with it. It should have been up three years ago. My poor cowman had a terrible time milking all the cows in the old place.' We found the cowman, wearing a rubber apron, busy in the dairy. Colonel Ashley introduced us and the cowman said that he'd got the six cows in a paddock close by. But first I was shown the two bulls in their pens.

'You can have the lot if you want them,' said the Colonel when we were in the paddock looking at the cows. 'For a very reasonable figure if you take the lot. These are all good, sound animals. I'm only selling them because I'm over-stocked. I've an eleven hundred gallon milk average, so I'm getting rid of all the cows that haven't given a thousand. There's one of these that regularly gives twelve hundred'. He pointed to a big, angular cow with rather an ugly pendulous udder, 'but she's not quite up to my standards of conformation. And—to tell you the truth—her butterfat's a bit low. A retailer has my milk and he has to compete with a man who runs a herd of Guernseys. But she could serve you well for several years, she's due in a month's time. Those two calved a few days ago.' He pointed his stick at them. 'And the other two calved a month ago. They've all given over nine hundred except that one.' He pointed. 'She's been a bit of a disappointment, she's never given quite nine hundred, but she's only a young cow, she's due in a month. And that one,' he pointed to a pretty young cow and glanced towards the milking shed behind us. In a lowered voice he continued, 'That one had her third calf a month ago, pedigree cow, plenty of milk behind her, she only gave seven hundred.' He lowered his voice still further, 'My cowman doesn't like her. The under cowman says he doesn't give her the proper ration of concentrates. She might do a lot better with you. Cowmen get these funny dislikes you know, there's nothing you can do about it. And Tom's a good cowman. And at the money I'm asking you can't lose. Why, I'd get almost as much for them barren.'

Back at the house, Colonel Ashley produced a patent shoe cleaner from under the seat in the porch and, after us-ing it, we went in, the Colonel still wearing his gumboots. He led me through a large entrance hall—in the middle of which stood a circular table with a big copper jug holding flowers, and a neatly folded copy of *The Times* upon it; along a stone flagged passage and into a spacious, well proportioned room with a high ceiling. 'I'll show you their milk records,' said Colonel Ashley, going to a bureau in a corner near a window. The windows of the room were almost to ground level and looked out over a park-like meadow with lime trees which were protected by iron railings; and the curtains were of rich gold brocade. Several oil paintings hung from the walls, a glass fronted book case against one wall, a Chippendale table stood in the centre of the room. While the Colonel fumbled at the bureau, I took note of the other furnishings so that I should be able to relate it all to Molly, the graceful Regency chairs and sofa, the lacquered corner cupboard with sparkling glass and dainty china, the flocked paper on the walls, the elegant sideboard with gleaming decanters and the thick carpet on which I stood.

While I was looking at the milk records, Colonel Ashley moved over to the sideboard, saying, 'I usually have a glass of sherry about this time,' and grasping a decanter he filled two glasses.

'I think you're very wise to buy all six cows,' he said as I sat at the bureau writing the cheque. 'Another sherry?' he said, when I handed him the cheque, but my eyes strayed to the French carriage clock and I said I must leave.

'Goodbye,' he called from the porch. 'Come and see me again after Christmas, I might have another cow or two for sale.'

I bought more cows, from a farmer who was getting old and giving up milking. One was a Friesian heifer close to calving; two were third calvers; the other two were older, but they were cheap and would help to fill another churn or two and thereby swell my monthly milk cheque. That was the great thing about milk, the regular cheque from the Milk Marketing Board. With other enterprises there was such a long wait for the money. From seed-time until harvest and beyond with corn, two years or more from calf to beef. Pigs were uncertain, you never knew with pigs; pigs were either right up or right down. Older farmers said there was either gold or copper in pigs. Fruit was a gamble, a late May frost could mean no crop. A good crop brought low prices, or in the case of a glut, no price at all. A poor crop meant high prices, but if you hadn't any fruit, it still meant no money. Sheep were steadier, and with few overhead costs—but only money twice a year, a cheque for wool and another for lambs, and one needed plenty of ground and good hedges.

Milk meant a cheque once a month. And milking meant bondage. A regular routine, milking twice a day, every day of the week, every week of the year. No matter what, cows had to be milked; world shattering events, health, anything, everything else became a poor second. Milking meant messing about with buckets, water and brushes; cleaning the dairy utensils, cleaning the cowshed. Feeding the cows—six months of the year seemed to be spent growing, gathering and storing food to feed them during the other six months. And yet, despite all, it was easy to grow very fond of cows; they are the nicest of creatures. Very few are bad-tempered by nature, they are trusting, placid animals on the whole. Fresh heifers can be wild, but with kindly treatment they usually settle down. Occasionally there's a really vicious one, but only very occasionally. Bad temper is usually caused by fear; good cowmen make good cows and bad cowmen make bad cows. In the wider sense of performance it's a longer and more heart breaking matter; one man's life being so short when it comes to breeding the perfect herd. Like farming itself, breeding a herd, having a uniform type of animal instead of just a collection, is 'a longish old job'.

That's why farmers need sons, so that the job begun can be handed on. But the road to a perfect herd is strewn with set-backs and disappointments, and a wrong bull used can be disastrous. It isn't as if it's just a matter of a good or bad bull. Even the best of bulls may fail to nick, as we say, with a particular herd, to nick meaning that the bull and cows produce consistently good offspring.

I made a start on the hedges. Father had made me a gift of hand tools from his shop; hedgebill, bill hook, an axe, a spade, shovels, manure and hay forks, hammers, an iron bar, ring beetle and other tools.

The sap was receding in the wood, making the hedges tough to cut. And unless I kept the hedgebill razor sharp the wood tended to peel, leaving the hedge unsightly. Not that it mattered so much today, many farmers had mechanical hedge trimmers that left the hedges in a shocking state, cracked, split and uneven. 'Bloody murder', Jack had commented on seeing such a hedge. 'Years ago it would've been a laughing stock, folk'd 'ave gyuled about it for months, but now they don't seem to care.'

Some of the hedges at Perrygrove were too high, it made cutting the top difficult; I had to strain upwards all the time. And because the hedges had not been cropped hard enough in previous years they were springy. Instead of standing firm as I cut them they 'ran away' as we called it. Of course, it was much easier just to nip the soft ends of the top and sides instead of the harder, more mature wood, but that way the hedges soon became loose and uncontrollable.

I decided just to trim the sides of the worst hedges and let them go up for a year or two and then lay them. The rest I returned to day after day, week after week—it's surprising how much hedging there can be on eighty acres, and you only realise how much when you trim them yourself. It is hard work, but I enjoyed it once I'd mastered the art. To the novice it is frustrating and worse, but fortunately I'd been well taught by Jack Musgrove at Suttridge. The secret is a sharp hedgebill of the right pattern, good strong strokes —and upward ones to avoid splitting the wood—you have to put effort into the work, and, I suppose, a good eye—to keep the tops level.

Yes, that autumn and during the early winter, I sweated at those hedges; even on frosty days and working in shirtsleeves. But I liked the work. It was good to pause, lean on the hedgebill and look back at chain after chain of neatly cropped hedge, with level top and smooth clean cuts. Day after day; I settled into a routine, how well I could understand the old farmworkers' liking for settling into a rut. And yet I knew it was dangerous for a farmer to settle into a rut; he had no boss to rout him out of it. So, after I'd cropped half the hedges, I ploughed the ley.

I'd almost finished the ploughing when Mr Saggamore came to view my progress. 'A pity', he said, 'you didn't persevere and get this ploughed earlier. If you'd planted it with Cappelle you'd have had a nice little cheque next year. It's a bit late now, you'd never get it broken down and planted before the rain comes.'

After milking by machine at Suttridge, I found hand milking at Perrygrove hard work. I'd lost the knack of sitting down beside a cow, a pail clasped between my knees, and easily coaxing milk from her udder. Instead of the robust ping as the first milk hit the pail bottom, my efforts only resulted in a feeble ting. And even when I'd succeeded in covering the bottom with three or four inches of milk there was none of that comfortable fuzz-fuzz-fuzz and the frothing of milk you get from the good quick twin jets of milk. My milk went slowly into the pail, thin squirts intermittently; and instead of a happy healthy looking froth, mine was flat and tired and sad looking. My wrists ached, I changed over teats and still they ached.

After a few days, I improved a little with the cows that had only been used to hand milking, and eventually managed the 'ping', the 'fuzz-fuzz-fuzz', and the froth, not much, but some at least. But even then, I was still rather slow; these cows moved their feet impatiently and turned their heads as much as to say, 'Not finished yet? How ever much longer will you be?'

With those cows that had only been used to a machine I remained as slow as ever. They didn't like this hand-milking any more than I did. Though, I must admit, I was beginning to enjoy milking the other cows, there's something pleasant about nuzzling your head into the ample flank of a cow in the morning, hearing that fuzz-fuzz-fuzz in the pail, feeling the increasing weight of milk between your knees. Turning your head slightly, cheek to warm cow, looking out through the window and watching the daylight strengthening and stealing overhead.

After I'd milked each cow, I tipped her milk into the weighing bucket hanging on the balance suspended from a beam. I entered her yield, in pounds, on the milk records sheet that was fastened to the wall. At roughly six week intervals the milk recorder would call, an afternoon and the following morning, remain while I milked, weigh the milk and take butterfat samples. A separate little red rubber stoppered bottle for each cow, into which milk from afternoon and morning would be put, together with two small yellow tablets to preserve the milk. These samples to be despatched in a locked metal box and sent by rail to the Milk Recording Society's laboratory. On his first visit, how long that poor Recorder had to wait for each cow's milk.

It was when two of the Clutterbuck cows had calved that I was later than usual into breakfast. 'I thought you were never coming this morning,' said Molly. 'The breakfast has been ready for ages, don't blame me if it's spoilt. What time you'll get in when those others have calved, goodness only knows.'

'I've got out of practice, that's what it is,' I replied, while Molly put the plates on the table. The bacon certainly did look a bit shrivelled. 'But I'm getting better. Quite a respectable froth this morning on Cowslips's milk, I thought.'

'I'm sure I could milk them in half the time,' said Molly as she poured coffee.

'It's Colonel Ashley's cows. They've never been used to hand-milking, they don't let their milk down very well. But they'll get used to it and so shall I. My wrists don't ache like they did.'

'Toast?' asked Molly a little later.

'Yes please. And while I think of it, couldn't we have a change of biscuits. Every time we have biscuits, it's those ginger things. Ever since we've been here we've had nothing but ginger biscuits. Even if you're fond of them, couldn't we have a change sometimes?'

'Fond of them? It's not me who's fond of them, it's you!'

'Me? Fond of ginger biscuits? Well, since you've said that I'll tell you something; I don't like ginger biscuits, and never have. Whatever made you think I was fond of them? Fond enough to have them every day, too.'

'Your mother told me. She said you liked to have a ginger biscuit every day.'

'I hate the things. I only ate them to please you.'

'I don't like them either. I only ate them because I thought you liked them,' said Molly.

'I wonder what made my Mother tell you that?'

'I don't know.'

'And the tapioca?' We'd had tapioca recently, stuff I detested.

'Yes. And the tapioca.' Molly by now could control her

laughter no longer. She started to clear the breakfast dishes while I lingered over a cup of coffee.

'Are you doing anything special this morning?' she asked.

'No. Not really. I was going hedge cropping, but it can wait. Why?'

'Well if you would go over to your father and get another milking stool, I could help you with the milking.'

'Are you sure?'

'Yes of course. Remember, I was hand-milking until a few weeks ago. The two of us will be much quicker.'

'I want a milking stool,' I told Father, when I got to the shop, 'but I'll go and see Mother first.' Mother was making pastry; slices of apple, peelings and cores lay on the kitchen table beside the pastry board. Looking hot and flustered, she glanced up as I stepped into the kitchen. 'Be careful with that door. Don't slam it. Close it gently. I've got a cake in the oven and if you slam the door it'll go down in the middle.'

I closed the door gently and walked towards the table where Mother was busy rolling out pastry, head bent over the rolling pin, she spoke without looking up. 'I thought when you left I'd have less to do. One less mouth to feed I thought. But I'm as busy as ever, on from morning to night. And that George is here every whipstitch eating me out of house and home.'

She stopped rolling pastry, wiped her floury hands on her apron and gave me a sharp look. 'How thin you're getting. Is Molly feeding you all right? Are you sure you're getting enough to eat? You look so thin to me. There's some little Welsh cakes in the cupboard, I'll give you a few to take back with you, there's plenty there. And I've just made some scones, they're over there cooling.' She pointed to a pile of scones on a plate on the dresser. 'You just sit down there

110

and I'll butter three or four. You can eat them together with a cup of nice hot Bovril.'

I assured Mother that I was getting plenty to eat, that Molly was an excellent cook and that I wasn't hungry at the moment.

'Oh yes,' she replied, still staring hard at me, 'you'd say that. You wouldn't admit that you're missing your Mother's cooking. Father always says what a good cook I am. And even that George says it, not that I take any notice of him! It's all soft soap with him, he only says it to wheedle more food out of me to ram down his great cannister.'

Mother resumed her pastry rolling. I watched her line the bowl, fill it with apple, and cap it with more pastry. After she'd trimmed the pastry round the bowl, she brushed the top of the pie with milk and popped it into the oven.

'There,' she said, carefully placing the cake she'd just taken from the oven on to a cooling tray, 'now we can have a nice cup of coffee.'

'Why,' I asked, as she was pouring the coffee, 'did you tell Molly that I was fond of ginger biscuits and tapioca?'

She put the tin of instant coffee powder back in the cupboard and replied, 'Because you are. When you were a little boy you loved ginger biscuits and tapioca pudding.'

'I came to get a milking stool. Molly's going to help me with the milking.'

'Is she? That's good of her. Oh, I do hope she'll make you a good wife. She seems a nice enough girl, so many girls today are so flighty, but I must say she seems nice enough, I really feel as if she's my daughter. But I can't see what she sees in that George.' Mother sniffed in a scornful way. 'I suppose he's over with you when he's not here or drinking himself silly at that Lion.'

'No. We don't see much of him.'

* * *

Uncle George was sitting in his garden shed, puffing at his pipe and with a mug of cider at his side.

'Ah, my boy', he greeted me, 'I'm doin' a bit of meditatin', but I've had a busy morning. That old fool of a Colonel was supposed to come and give me a hand, but he never turned up, so I had to turn round and do everything meself. Then I had Higgins' (the doctor) 'down here wanting a bit of advice. He's goin' to keep a pig or two and wanted to know how to set about it and so on. Hindered me a bit, but I didn't mind, he's a good old sort. It shows he's got his head screwed on right, havin' the sense to come to me for advice. Very different from Alfred Tucker' (the butcher) 'he's bought that six acres and intends to keep a herd of breeding sows. He thinks he knows it all, he'd never have the sense to come to me for advice. And what does he know about pig breeding? Ask yerself a question, what do Alfred Tucker know about pig breeding—bugger all! Never mind, let him get on with it. Have a drop of cider and forget all about him. Tell Molly I'll bring them pullets over in a few days time. By gum, ain't they a picture, got combs on 'em like sunsets. They want to be moved now or they'll be layin' and the move will upset 'em. I don't mind Molly havin' some of 'em, but I ain't lettin' anybody have birds like that. But I am goin' to keep less stock in future. I'm goin' to ease up a bit. At my time of life I can't keep goin' hammer and tongs, day after day, out in all winds and weather.'

That afternoon Molly sat on the new stool and helped me milk the cows. To my chagrin, she milked two cows to my one.

CHAPTER TEN

Neighbours

A week later, after two more cows had calved, and while I was hedge-cropping my neighbour, Mr Wrenn, came by. 'Got any more cows to calve?' he asked, looking over the hedge at my fourteen milkers in the field. 'Another two shortly,' I replied.

'You want to get a milking machine,' he said. 'Save a lot of work. I used to milk by hand and then my man was ill for a time and I had to milk the lot myself. After about three weeks I went into breakfast one morning and said to my missus, I'm off to town to order a milking machine. I'd had enough of it, milking the lot by myself every morning. At night the missus gave me a hand as best she could, but in the

113

mornings she was busy, giving the kids their breakfast and getting them off to school; they were only little ones then. You want to get off today and see about one, you'll never regret it.'

I said I'd been thinking about it.

'Yes,' he said, 'you get off and get one. You'll need one with more cows. Milk's the thing to go in for, regular monthly cheque coming in. Milk's far and away the best thing for chaps like us, with our acreage and type of ground. Milk's a good steady thing today, not like it was when I started. There wasn't any Milk Marketing Board in those days. Once a year I had to go and line up with a lot of other farmers and wait to get a contract. We damn near had to fight for a contract. At milk less than sixpence a gallon. You wouldn't believe it today would you?'

We were a dairy district; almost every farm, except some of the smallest, had a herd of milking cows. I rather envied some of these small men their independence, their easy going way of life. However, in these times of peace and promised prosperity it was becoming increasingly difficult for a married man with a family to make a living on twenty or thirty acres. The system whereby a man combined small-holding with some other business or trade seemed to be dying out. Consequently, most of these small places were now occupied by middle-aged or elderly men. Some were muddle men, it was a mystery how they existed, but the majority took a pride in their holdings. Orchards well cared for, neat yards and buildings. They loved tarring their gates, fences, sheds. The tar on the sheds, after years of generous successive applications, was glossy, cracked and curtained from its thickness and the heat of the sun.

One of these black betarred sheds, or possibly some brick-built and pantiled shed, was probably a cider house, and it was here that the older men seemed to spend most of their time. Time appeared to be a commodity they had in plenty, and in the company of a crony or two they would beguile it by passing the cider mug round and talking of times past. From the recesses of their minds they drew forth the memories of a golden age. Real or imaginary, they lived again those wondrous times. Hardships, though not minimised, acquired a lustre and became glories instead. Gargantuan pigs and cattle grew even bigger as the cider mug was passed round and round again. Prodigious feats of strength were remembered; bountiful crops of corn, hay, roots and fruit were harvested again. If memory should fade, or silence elapse, further inspiration was sought, and it was soon forthcoming in the tart, amber liquid in the grimy communal mug. Summers were better, winters harder in the days of their youth. Lips would be smacked and heads shaken at the very wonder of it all; of men, cattle, scenes, all rekindled in fond memory and a refill at the cask. The changes they had witnessed; changes on the whole to be deplored; progress viewed with suspicion.

Most of these men lived frugal lives, money was for saving not spending. They repaired, patched, made do; produced much of their food and drink. The well stocked garden that put many a farm garden to shame, the bacon pig in the cot, the several barrels of cider and perry. Economy is of itself a great revenue, said Cicero, and thus lived these men; soon they and their kind would be memories only.

Victor Lewis, another of my neighbours, also had this peasant temperament, living frugally, valuing his independence; hating officialdom, forms, restrictions and regulations, but because his acreage was larger and because he had a number of milking cows, he had to conform. But it was obvious he found it irksome.

Victor was a hefty man, with a face as red as the setting sun on a frosty night, contrasting oddly with his blue eyes and his straw coloured hair and eyebrows; thick bushy eyebrows that came down over his eyes like thatch. He wore a battered old trilby hat, covered in grease and cow hair, a long khaki smock with twine tied round it. He swore and shouted a lot. Early in the mornings I could hear his strong, deep voice, calling the cows to milking. 'C'mon, C'mon, C'mon home, you buggers.'

Victor's wife had a red face, and black, unruly hair. She also had a number of unruly children. Victor said he wasn't going to pay a lot of tax, he was going to have a lot of kids instead. His father and mother lived with them in the dilapidated half-timbered farmhouse and Victor said they spoilt the children. 'If I threaten to lay a hand on 'em, they rush off to Gramp. He makes such a fuss of 'em, won't let me touch 'em. He weren't like that when I was a young un, many's the time he've put his belt round me and my brothers.'

Victor attended all the farm sales, in greasy hat and khaki smock, buying 'stuff that might come in useful'. He wasn't a proud or fussy man; I don't think he cared a jot what people thought of him. Among the brambles and stinging nettles in his rickyard could be found a wonderful collection of old wagons, carts, implements, tractors and tools, all of them in a state of disrepair, bought cheaply because they were broken and bought because they might come in handy one day.

Robert Windrush over at Fairfield Farm was very different from Victor Lewis. He was one of the new men in farming; young, educated, tall and good looking. Efficiency was his watchword. He made it quite plain that he had no time for the old ways of farming. Farming was, he declared, a business, an industry just like any other industry.

He'd bought Fairfield Farm from the Darcy family just after the war had ended. He was now in the process of joining farm to farm—I think he'd just bought his third —selling off the farmhouses, pulling out orchards and grubbing-up hedges. Hedges were wasteful and inefficient in his opinion; they occupied land that could be growing crops and never brought in a penny return.

But Robert Windrush, despite all the head shaking, the muttering of, 'it'll never last, you can't farm like that, farming is a longish old job', was successful. The number of milk churns on the stand was proof of that. Like all farmers, I counted the churns at every farm.

Windrush spent freely—invested was his word—on cattle, buildings, installations, machinery and fertilisers. Not only were hedges and orchards grubbed-out, but trees were felled and their roots removed; they impeded machinery and took up valuable space. Fields were drained, ditches were piped and filled in. He calculated how much ground he'd gained for growing grass. Grass was his only crop, grass for grazing, for silage and hay. Simple ley mixtures of rye grass and white clover, he had no time for the old permanent pastures composed of many species of grasses, clovers and herbs. Herbage, the old farmers called it, 'Weeds', retorted Windrush. Cows were his only stock; cows and their followers, that is young stock bred for replacements.

You had to hand it to him, he was effiicient and successful, and his workmen were better paid than most. There weren't many of them, and—so it was said—he timed them with a stop watch.

The Darcys, brother and two sisters, all unmarried and elderly, still lived in the farmhouse. Mr Darcy had an old Austin Seven, and though by no means a fast driver his driving was both erratic and dangerous. The car chugged along, jumped along, or roared along in bottom gear, veering from side to side with an apprenhensive looking Mr Darcy at the wheel. Seeing him set the car in motion had always an element of surprise. Sometimes the car would stall, at other times it would shoot off with the engine at full throttle; but no one knew, least of all Mr Darcy, whether it would move forwards or backwards. It was advisable to stand well clear when Mr Darcy was in his motor—and sometimes when he wasn't; Mr Darcy was very forgetful about the hand-brake.

The Darcys were quiet, shy, gentle people. 'We like to keep ourselves to ourselves', they used to say. But for all that they seemed to know and be known by people from all over the county. We were accepted by them because they knew my family, had known my grandparents. 'We like to know who people are, know their background. We don't like these fly-by-nights', they said. They could have added, though they didn't, that a few generations in local churchyards were also part of a person's credentials.

Our nearest village was almost a mile to the south, though you'd scarcely call it a village. Just a score or so of scattered houses, a small church, a school now closed but occasionally used for village functions, a post office and a pub called The Queens' Head. The village hadn't a resident clergyman, but the vicar of a neighbouring parish held services there once a fortnight. Well, in theory he did, but according to Mrs Gymble, 'it all depended'. Apparently he waited outside the church in his motor car and if nobody had arrived five minutes after the service was supposed to begin he drove away.

When we first came to Perrygrove, Mrs Gymble had told us that we could 'get all sorts at the Post Office'. However, we soon found it was difficult to get anything at all; even stamps were sold with reluctance. An elderly, bent-up woman with a 'nutcracker' face kept the place. She walked with the aid of a stick and had a shrill voice. 'I hope you haven't come for oil', she said on our first visit, 'because I don't want to take on any new customers, I'm running that side of the business down, it's more caddle than it's worth.'

She seemed to be running down other sides of the business too. 'I don't mind letting you have a few other things as long as you don't come too often,' she said. But looking round the shop we saw few other things. A dank, depressing smell clung to the little room, I wondered how she prevented the postage stamps sticking together in such an atmosphere. 'You could have a packet of cigarettes or baccy occasionally,' she volunteered. 'There's some as always gets their baccy from here, they says they lets it get too dry at the public, when you opens it a puff of wind and pooph! it's all gone, they says.'

The Queens Head was kept by Elijah Podsnap and his wife. Elijah was an elderly, grisly little man with a wispy beard. Every time I'd seen him he was wearing a cap, a thick woollen cardigan, Derby tweed breeches with the laces beneath the knees undone, and carpet slippers. He spent his time sitting in the fireside corner or playing quoits. When a customer entered or needed service he shouted, 'Missus, Missus'. If Mrs Podsnap did not appear within a second or two he would go and rap on the counter and shout, 'Missus, Missus, custom. Missus, where are you? Get a move on, there's a customer waiting.'

Mrs Podsnap would lollop into sight, making half-humming, half-singing noises. She was very thin, her fingers were red and knotted, and her hair was pulled back tightly into a bun. Podsnap kept the poor old lady going backwards and forwards, drawing beer from a barrel in a room behind. Yet she never seemed to mind, she seemed cheerful and kept on making that humming-singing noise as she lolloped back and forth.

The ceiling of the bar was low and stained almost black by tobacco smoke. The flagstones on the floor were bare; the place was stark, some benches round the walls, a shove halfpenny board on the counter, a quoit board on a table, two other rickety tables and a few wooden chairs. Behind the counter were cupboards and beneath them some shelves with jars of animal ointment and, in the autumn, marrows, apples, onions and potatoes.

There was another room with an old piano, and paper that was sagging and peeling from the walls; damp and fusty and rarely used. One night, however, about a month after we'd moved to Perrygrove, I noticed a solitary figure in there who seemed vaguely familiar. 'Who's that in the other room?' I asked.

'That Bill Lugg,' replied Podsnap. 'He've taken to coming here most nights and sitting in there alone. Sometimes Mrs Tunney do go in and have a word with him. I won't have her in here, I make her stay out in the passage. I don't really like her goin' in that other room either. I wish she wouldn't come here, she's a dangerous woman.'

I knew Mrs Tunney; she'd been porter at the railway halt during the war. I could think of several adjectives that might be applied to Mrs Tunney; rough, tough, formidable, awkward, drunken or foulmouthed; or kind, genial, generous or lively; but not dangerous.

'Dangerous?' I asked.

'Ah, dangerous,' replied Podsnap, stroking his beard, and then giving it a little tug as if to reassure himself that it wasn't a false one. 'Ah, dangerous,' he repeated. 'Her do come in here, a woman on her own, and sit down and start chatting to anybody as do come, showing her bloomers and with her legs wide apart for any man, and what do that mean, eh? One chap followed her out one night and, so he told us after, he only just put his hand up her skirt, you know, thinkin' he was all right after what he'd seen in here. And her played merry hell, threatened to report him and make a case on't and all. I don't want none of that gwaine on in my place, so I've kept her out of here since. Mind, if Bill Lugg do care to take her off from here an' slip it up her, that's no business of mine, but I don't want none of that here.'

I went into the other room; I soon saw why I hadn't recognised Bill. His hair was plastered down with hair oil, he wore a cheap, badly fitting blue suit with the lapels of the jacket curled, his customary khaki shirt now buttoned to the neck and with a dreadful bright yellow tie. He was sitting rather ill at ease, a cigarette in his mouth and looking miserable.

120

'Hello, Bill'

' 'Ullo,' he replied glumly, and then looking up and seeing me, he grinned and said,' 'ow be you, then?'

'What are you doing here?' I asked. It was some way from his home.

'Courtin',' he answered in a dreary, matter of fact way.

'Who? Not Mrs Tunney?'

'No. But I did think about 'er some while back, aye I did. But I decided to gie 'er the go-by. Aye, I did. 'Er said summat I didn't much care for, aye 'er did.'

This was a bit of a surprise. Bill always said he didn't hold with marriage, he believed it took all the marrow out of a man's bones.

'I never thought you'd ever marry, Bill.'

'No more did I. But since our mother died, I've got lonely like. No comfort, our Grit's no company, allus off out and I've got tired of doin' the cookin' an' all, aye I 'ave.'

'Who's your girl friend then?'

'Olive Cox. 'Er's a nice sized 'oman, aye 'er is.' Olive Cox lived quite close to The Queens Head. As Bill said, she was a nice sized woman, a woman who looked like a well filled bolster.

'So you meet her here.'

'Well, no, not exackly. 'Er an't met me yer yet, no 'er an't. But I look at it this way, 'er's bound to come yer some time or other, 'er do live 'andy. And where else would 'er get a packut of fags? 'Er do smoke like a chimmuck, that I do know, aye I do. 'Er's bound to come in yer on the off chance like or summat, it do stand to reason, aye it do.'

I bought him a pint of beer, but even this didn't cheer him up.

'Well,' I said as I left, 'good luck, Bill.'

'Ah,' he said, with a wan grin, 'but it's a bit of a caper this courtin', aye it be.'

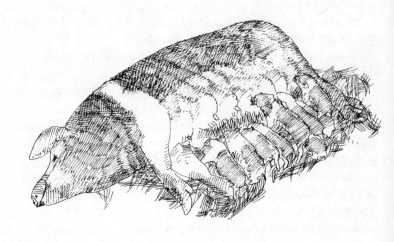

CHAPTER ELEVEN

'It happens to us all, lad'

The third and last of the sows farrowed, taking me unawares. In the cot one morning I found the sow lying on her side in a nest of straw and nine silky little pigs with crinkled pink snouts all busy sucking and tugging at her teats. The sow half lifted her head, flicked aside a big flop ear and gazed at me steadily with one eye before settling back with a grunt of deep contentment.

The other two litters of pigs were growing, scrambling and muddling in their mothers' troughs at feeding time. And during the day time they accompanied their mothers in the orchard; scampering, snuffling, squeaking, making immature grunts, skidding and running into each other and thoroughly enjoying life. Alarming the black and white speckled pullets.

When undisturbed, the pullets strolled majestically about the orchard, their bright enquiring eyes alert for worm or grub. A large find of tempting tit-bits was heralded by much squawking, a gathering call, invitation to the others to come and share the bounty. They came running with outstretched legs; eager beaks would shoot down snapping up the food, accompanied by a happy chattering; keen claws would scratch, legs kicking backwards, heads bobbing, feathers fluffed. Until, attracted by the noise, the little pigs came charging. The pullets scattered, frightened, affronted and indignant. From a distance, a safe distance, they viewed the piglets with baleful eyes. Unconcerned, the piglets would rootle happily in the turf and the sows would rush to join them with ear-flapping, udder-swaying alacrity.

Three of Colonel Ashley's cows calved, two of them had bull calves, but the other, Buttercup, the one that Colonel Ashley had found a bit disappointing, had a heifer. The day after Buttercup calved—she had a large udder and looked like milking well—she became unsteady on her feet, swaying in a drunken manner and eventually collapsing on the ground. I propped her up with some bales of straw—lying prone there was a danger of her becoming 'blown'—and rushed off to telephone the Vet.

'She's got milk fever,' I told him.

'Right!' he replied, 'I'll come straight away. There's a lot of it about this year.'

Milk fever is a fall of calcium in the blood. Fever, though, is a misnomer, and the cow goes into a coma; it can be fatal if not caught in time. It occurs just after calving, occasionally before, most often in the autumn and nearly always to the higher yielding cows. The treatment used to be milking out the udder and then inflating it with a bicycle pump, but now injections of calcium are given and no milk is taken from the udder.

I hadn't long to wait for the Vet, fortunately I'd caught him at his surgery. With milk fever as with a difficult calving or with bloat, speed is essential.

It was Mr Carmichael, who came. A sparely built man, of about fifty years of age. 'Where is she?' he asked jumping out of his car and without wasting any words on preliminaries.

'In the loose box.'

'Good, always better if they're in,' he said, getting his equipment out of the boot of the car.

He gave her two bottles of calcium, one in the blood-stream for immediate effect and one just under the skin which should complete the cure. He held the upturned bottles high above the prostrate cow and the liquid ran down a tube into her. 'She's not too bad, caught in good time, she should be up soon.'

The effect was miraculous, soon the cow began to show an interest in life again. She began to struggle and in no time at all was on her feet, 'She should be all right now,' he said as he walked back to his car and stowed his stuff away in the back. 'Keep an eye on her,' he said as he slammed the door, waved goodbye and drove away.

I continued with my hedge cropping, the ground was dry; the winter corn was up in drill, no blank spaces and the rows were straight. That was good, I didn't want my neighbours looking over the hedge to see crooked rows or places I'd missed, and to hear them making remarks about dogs' hind legs or casually say that somebody needed spectacles.

'Wonderful weather,' said our new friend the postman one morning, 'I hope it lasts.'

But a couple of days later it rained. We had three days of

solid driving rain. Rain gushed from the roof tops, the guttering and drain pipes full, the drains gurgled. At night our windows rattled as the rain slashed against them. The fields squelched, puddles forming in the imprints made by the cows' hooves. The cows began to hang in the gateways, waiting to come in at milking time. They knew that hay awaited them in the racks; and where they stood became a morass of mud.

A blustery day. The sun shone fitfully, shyly, as if ashamed of its long absence. I saw Mrs Gymble as I was walking past her cottage, hanging up washing, her mouth full of pegs. She took the pegs from her mouth and turned to me.

'I missed the buz into town yesterday', she said. 'I had to wait an hour for another one. I had to go. That's why I'm doing my washing today. And coming back home I got drenched, it's a long trek back up from that buz. I don't know, we got nothing here, no 'lectricity, they've got it everywhere else. No water but what we wind up from the well. And over a mile and a half to walk to a buz or a train. I said to my Fred, we oughta pack up and move to somewhere where they've got it all. You could easily get another job I said, they'd be glad of a chap like you who'd be prepared to put his back into it. Half of 'em today wun't work, not to put their backs into it like what he do. But Fred, he wun't shift. No, he says, what's the sense in moving at our time of life, Alice. He wouldn't take a chance you see. My people would have helped him, my father had a small farm and I'd always been used to the work when I was a girl. But he wouldn't do it, he prefers working for wages, no ambition you see.'

She started hanging up more clothes, but went on talking. 'That's the trouble with Fred, he's a good husband, nobody could have a better, but he's got no ambition. He could have

125

taken a little farm once, but he wouldn't. "Better not risk it, Alice," he said, "we're all right as we are."'

I found some bags of minerals and several cardboard boxes back at the farmhouse. 'The railway lorry brought that lot' Molly told me. 'I thought you'd only ordered a few bags of minerals and half-a-dozen bottles of stuff from that man Tinkerpoof.'

'So did I', I said, opening the boxes, 'but look here, bottles of *CHILLOWAY, DANDY, AFTERCALFO, BURPO*, packets of *HISEXY, WORMYGO, PHIZZ-PHIZZ*, and some tins of ointment and udder cream. I didn't order all this stuff, and I'm not having it. After I've done the milking I'll go down to the 'phone box and speak to old Tinkerpoof.'

Tinkerpoof was delighted to hear from me. 'Yes, yes', he said, 'don't hesitate to ring me at any time. That's what I've got the telephone for. Now, how can I help you?'

'It's about that stuff of yours that came to-day. I ...'

'Only arrived today? It's the railway, they're very slow. I'll speak to them about it, but I didn't think any of it was urgent. If I'd known, I'd have ...'

I cut in quickly, it was the only way with Tinkerpoof. 'I never ordered all that stuff ...'

'What? What did you say? I thought you ...'

I spoke louder and more firmly. 'I said I never ordered all that stuff. And what's more, I don't want it.'

'Never ordered it? Don't want it?' Tinkerpoof sounded incredulous.

'I'll pay for what I ordered, but the rest of it I want taken away.'

Tinkerpoof was now making strange noises. I thought he wasn't going to speak again and was about to say goodbye when suddenly, 'You must excuse me', came a sad voice, 'but I'm quite upset.' More strange noises issued from the telephone, I began to think he might be sobbing. 'I'm quite overcome, quite upset, never had this happen before.' The words came in gasps. 'I don't know what to say, you've really upset me. I was only trying to help you, it's all stuff you'll need. Nobody's ever treated me like this before, I must have time to think.' The pips went and I put more money in the coin box.

'Hullo, you still there?' Tinkerpoof's voice was back to normal. 'You pay for the stuff, keep what you need and use any of the other stuff you want to and I'll call round in a month or two and pick the rest up and refund you.'

Tinkerpoof never called in a month or in two, and neither did he call the following year. We never saw him again.

The bucket fed calves were drinking well now, but it hadn't been like that in the beginning. When I'd first taken them away from their mothers, I thought they'd never learn to drink milk from a bucket. No wonder Mr Saggamore had reared his calves on cows, though that too had been difficult at times. There were occasions when the nurse cow would refuse to take to a strange calf and would kick out, sending the poor unfortunate calf flying across the shed. A strap or cord would then be tied round the recalcitrant cow to restrain her until she'd accepted the calf or calves.

But teaching the calves to put their heads down to drink was against their natural instinct of putting their heads up to suck. With the calf backed into a corner, a finger in its mouth and the rest of the hand forcing its muzzle down into a bucket of milk held in the other hand, it was a matter of luck and patience. Often the calf would refuse; the milk got cold. The hand holding the bucket had to be on the alert lest the calf should suddenly bunt and send the milk and bucket flying.

'You want to use some of our milk substitute for feeding those calves,' said the man from The Farmers' Stores. 'You'll find it a lot cheaper than whole milk.' But I preferred to use cows' milk; after all it was intended to be the food for calves, and even if it were dearer I didn't have to part with any hard cash.

This first batch of calves were growing too; each week showed a difference. All legs, and eyes and ears, they looked pretty in the shed. Now I had another three calves to teach to drink.

'You'll soon be stocked up,' said Mr Wrenn, 'if you're going to keep all the bull calves as well as the heifers.'

I had occasion to call on Mr Wrenn late one evening. The Friesian heifer was trying to calve and she was obviously in difficulties. After I'd examined the heifer, I said to Molly, 'The calf's the wrong way round, I'll have to 'phone the vet.'

'Go to Mr Wrenn,' said Molly, 'that's the nearest telephone.'

The vet promised to come immediately. I offered Mr Wrenn the money for the call. 'No, I won't take anything for that, but I'd better come with you, and my boy will. I'll give him a shout, he's in the other room. You never know you may need a lot of help.' He went off and I heard him calling, 'David! David! They want some help at Perrygrove, they've got a difficult calving.'

'Right,' said Mr Carmichael, after he'd pulled on his high wader-like boots, donned his rubber calving apron and tied the tapes behind his neck; his bare elbows appeared pointed and red in the light of the hurricane lantern. We filed towards the loose-box, Mr Wrenn, short and stocky, carrying the hurricane lantern, David Wrenn, a younger edition of his father, carrying a calving rope. Mr Carmichael clumping along in his boots and carrying his equipment, and me with a bucket of warm water and soap, and a towel slung round my shoulders.

Mr Wrenn hung the lantern from a beam and I fastened

the chain dangling from the manger round the heifer's neck. 'Make sure that she can go down if she wants to,' cautioned Mr Carmichael, busy smearing antiseptic ointment on to his bare arms. David held the heifer's tail and Mr Carmichael gently inserted his arm to its full length and stood there with his shoulder tight against the heifer's rump. 'We're going to have a job', he said, 'she's got two, round the wrong way and all tangled up.'

After a while the heifer lay down. It was a cold night, but Mr Carmichael, lying full length in the straw, soon had his face wet with perspiration. 'I can't quite ...' he said. 'The calves are so tangled, it'll take a long time.' An hour went by, there wasn't much we could do but watch the breathless, struggling vet, grunting and sweating behind the heifer. The heifer lay still, giving an occasional low moan and looking at us with her gentle trusting eyes.

'This doesn't happen very often,' said Mr Carmichael, standing up now. 'I know an old trick, it sometimes works. We'll roll her right over, it might shift the calves and then I may be able to pull this one free.'

We rolled the heifer over, the vet inserted his arm again. 'I think that's done it,' he said. Ten minutes later we rolled the unprotesting heifer again. Eventually, the vet produced a leg, a hind one and then another. We fixed a rope to each leg. 'I hope we've the right ones, if not we're in trouble. Now, you can pull gently.'

While we were pulling and Mr Carmichael was manipulating the calf inside, Mr Wrenn said, 'I've known some to be terrible cruel at this job. I knew a man once who tied the calves legs to a motor car.'

'Harder now,' instructed the Vet, 'keep up a good steady pull.'

'The calves will be dead, I suppose,' said David.

'I expect both of them will be,' replied the Vet, 'I thought at one time I'd have to cut them out.'

'Keeping the heifer alive, that's the main thing,' said Mr Wrenn.

The calf came quickly at the end, making me tumble over backwards, the sudden easing of any resistance on the ropes. 'Now for the other one,' Mr Carmichael said, his hand inside the heifer. 'This should be easier,' and to the cow, 'Not long now, old girl.'

Ten minutes later the other calf lay stretched and lifeless on the straw. The vet attended to the heifer. Mr Wrenn looked down at the two dead calves, one a bull, the other a heifer. 'That heifer would never have bred,' he said, 'even if she'd lived. A twin to a bull never does.' Mr Carmichael washed his arms and dried them, then tipped the soapy disinfected water down his apron. We trouped back to the car and he removed his apron and long rubber boots and stowed them in the boot of the car with his other equipment, then put his shoes and coat on.

I thanked them all and asked them in for a drink, which they declined because it was so late.

'She won't get up until tomorrow,' Mr Carmichael said, 'she's had a rough time.'

'It's tomorrow already,' said Mr Wrenn, holding his pocket watch to the lantern, 'It's gone midnight.'

'Give me a ring if you're worried about her,' called the vet as he drove away.

I thanked Mr Wrenn and David again. 'Any time, lad, don't hesitate,' said Mr Wrenn. 'Any time,' echoed David.

Next morning we telephoned Mr Carmichael to thank him, and he asked how the heifer was.

'Fine, she's up and about and eating, you'd never think she'd had any trouble.'

'She's a damn sight better than me then, we both had a rough time and I'm feeling the effects of it even if she isn't,' he said.

It wasn't long before I was calling the vet again; this was, I was to find, a common pattern. Have the vet once and you seemed to be having him almost every day. Troubles went in cycles—mine seemed to be a continuous cycle in those early months. We began to get worried; it became a kind of grim hanging on, but then that's part of the art of farming, the ability to hang on. It is the test of the real farmer; he may worry and grumble but he tightens his belt and with a stubborn fortitude he hangs on, even to the point of going bust. It's the outsiders, the men with a bit of money who come into farming thinking it's an easy way to make more; they're the ones who chuck up when trouble arises.

Early one morning I found Strawberry under the hedge in a corner of the paddock. She was due to calve in four days time. Late the previous night she'd shown no sign of calving, but now she was flat on the ground, obviously in distress. She was unable to rise, her shoulders and back were wet with sweat and her head was covered with earth from her feeble struggling.

'I was still in bed when you rang', said Mr Carmichael. 'I expect it's milk fever. Nasty when it comes on before calving because it so often takes you unawares. We'd better take some warm water, soap, and towels with us, in case she doesn't get up. And if she's opened up enough we'll get the calf away—there's always the danger of a dead calf in these cases.'

I'd already propped the cow up with some bales of straw and covered her with some sacks, but when we reached her the bales had been pushed aside, most of the sacks had fallen off and the cow was lying stretched out with her legs extended and stiff. 'It's milk fever all right,' Mr Carmichael said after a few seconds. 'We'll get her into a better position and then I'll give her a couple of bottles of calcium.' He examined her and found her too closed to calve. 'We'll have to leave her,' he said.

We waited for the calcium to take effect, but this time there was no response. 'Keep her propped up, and well covered as well,' he advised. 'And if she's not up by dinner time give me another ring.'

The cow wasn't up by one o'clock. Carmichael saw her again just after two. 'She doesn't look as if she'll get up today, you'd better get her inside. It's cold at night now and there's a danger of pneumonia,' he said.

'Keep her warm,' he instructed, just before leaving. 'I'll be along in the morning and we'll have to get the calf away.'

Mr Wrenn and David helped me to get the cow into a shed; we rolled her on to a gate which we dragged behind the tractor. We pushed, lifted and heaved, and managed to bundle her inside where we propped her up with bales of straw and covered her with sacks. Next morning Mr Carmichael gave her more calcium but still no response; we got the calf away; 'Still alive,' he said, blowing into its mouth and massaging it. 'That's lucky, I thought it might be dead.' He shook a thermometer and pushed it into the cow's anus, then he put a stethoscope to his ears and listened to her heart. After removing the thermometer he wiped it and looked at it. 'She's got a high temperature and her heart's not too good.' He slapped the cow hard on her rump three or four times, the last slap also drove in the needle of his syringe. 'Antibiotics,' he explained as he fixed syringe to needle and pressed the plunger. 'I'll be along tomorrow morning. There's not much more we can do now, but ring me if she seems worse.'

I kept watch and once during the night I found her lying flat again. Molly and I managed to get her upright—and a helpless cow takes some heaving—and propped her up again. She'd got blown lying flat, but not enough to be serious.

'I don't like the look of her,' said Carmichael next morning, after examining her and giving her antibiotics.

'She's still got a high temperature, her breathing's not good and I don't like the sound of her heart. I don't like to give her any more calcium because of her heart. Keep her warm and give her a pint of strong black coffee three times a day. Be careful how you drench her, she'd choke very easily. I'll look in again tomorrow.'

He called daily, sometimes giving the cow an injection; always examining her with his stethoscope and taking her temperature. The cow became weaker, listless, hardly bothering to glance at us with her poor, tired, troubled eyes. Carmichael gave little hope for her, telling me to keep up the doses of strong coffee. On the fifth or sixth day he said, 'We'll give her one more day. I'll call tomorrow and give her a different injection and we'll try to get her up. Get some help here.'

On the following day, Mr Wrenn and David were present when he arrived. 'I'll give her an injection,' he said, after examining her. 'It's a risk, but she may respond and if she does we may be able to get her on her feet. She can't go on like this. Are you willing to take the risk?'

I looked at Mr Wrenn who nodded. 'Yes,' I said.

The cow did not even flinch when the hypodermic needle was plunged into her neck; her lack lustre eyes never blinked.

'She's going,' said Mr Carmichael, and the cow's head flopped, lifeless. 'It was her heart', he explained. 'I'm sorry, but there was nothing I could do.'

'You're having the same bad luck as I had when I first started,' said Mr Wrenn. 'I had a cow die within a few weeks of starting on my own. I said to old Fred, who'd worked on the farm ever since he was a boy, "Where can we bury her?" and he said, "Anywhere. You can bury a cow anywhere on this farm." I felt a bit better when he said that, because people had been saying to me, "Fancy taking a young wife and baby to a poor old farm like that." But when I knew a cow could be buried anywhere on the farm I knew the farm couldn't be so bad as people made out. But it's bad luck, lad, losing a cow like that just when you're starting. It's a terrible set-back. It makes you feel bad, but you'll feel better in a few days. I know, because I've been through it. Folk who say they've never had any losses are bloody liars. When you keep livestock, you'll have deadstock. It happens to us all, lad.'

CHAPTER TWELVE

Back-end of the Year

Molly believed that a well kept flower garden was a mark of civilisation and as necessary to the heart as vegetables were to the stomach.

'Two or three days' work will make the world of difference,' she said at breakfast one morning, 'and Colonel's coming to help.' Surprisingly, Colonel did come and together we cleared the brambles, the elder and the clumps of nettles.

Molly's enthusiasm also met with Uncle George's approval. 'I like to see a woman tending her garden. My mother allus liked her flowers. Never could understand why Ethel didn't take more interest. Aggie ain't got much of a garden

135

to speak of, but she ain't got the room. They 'aven't even got the room for a vegetable garden. Not as it's much odds, that old Sam 'ould never put a spade in't if they 'ad. Lazy old varmint. Just sit there, day atter day, eatin' an' drinkin' an' gruntin'. "Why dussent stir thyself, Sam?" I asks'n. But not 'im, allus the same. And our Aggie do fuss an' run round 'im, an' 'e ain't worth it. 'E's no bottle, never was, but Aggie do seem to like'n.'

Molly had planted snowdrops, crocuses, daffodils and tulips and now I planted a lilac, some bush roses and a red hawthorn tree. 'We'll need a lot more shrubs,' said Molly. 'And in the spring I'll plant hollyhocks, columbines, paeonies, pinks, delphiniums and lupins and lots more. But we must get some more shrubs now.'

I didn't know if Molly had made subtle hints, but during the next few weeks Mrs Gymble brought some shrubs her Fred had grown. Colonel brought a Maiden's Blush rose bush and then Uncle George arrived with a collection of shrubs.

It was Uncle George who brought the geese. Three geese and a gander. 'Why have you brought those things here?' I asked. I hated geese and feared them a little as well. 'Molly wanted 'em,' said Uncle George. 'A woman wants a few geese and things. My old mother allus liked 'er poultry, allus 'ad a fair few ducks an' geese an' 'ens round 'er. An' Molly do need 'em just the same.'

'You never said a word to me about those geese,' I said to Molly, after Uncle George had left.

'No,' replied Molly, stoutly, 'I thought you might object.'

'I would have. I do object.'

'That's what I thought, that's why I didn't say.'

'I call it an underhand way of going on.'

'And so do I,' answered Molly, smiling. 'Now, don't be so grumpy about it. I've got a surprise for you, you've been asking for tripe and onions and I've cooked some for your dinner.'

'Do you like it?' Molly asked at dinner time. And a few minutes later she asked again.

'Well,' I replied slowly, 'since you ask, it's not as good as my mother's. You'd better ask her how to cook tripe.'

'Oh! Should I!' said Molly, her eyes blazing. 'If that's how you feel you can go to your mother and eat tripe, 'cos you won't get any more here. How dare you sit there and say that to me! Don't eat it. I don't want you to make yourself ill.' She jumped up and snatched the plate from me. I tried to make amends, but Molly would have none of it. 'Don't speak to me,' she said, her anger turning to sorrow. I noticed tears forming in the corners of her eyes.

'I'm sorry. I didn't mean—'

'Oh yes, you did—don't dare speak to me.'

And I didn't—until tea time. But I never made that mistake again.

There was the affair about the cats, however. Looking at our hearth in the living room, with its big open fire, I realised something was missing. We needed a cat, prefer- ably a large black cat, who would sit there purring and so complete the domestic scene. 'We need a cat', I said to Molly, 'a cat would look nice sitting there beside the fire.'

'I'm not having a cat in the house,' said Molly.

'It would catch the mice,' Molly was frightened of mice and I felt that this would clinch the argument. Already in my mind's eye I could see a sleek, fat, purring cat beside the fire. Actually, I knew where just such a cat could be obtained.

'You can have a cat outside if you wish—as long as I don't have it near me, but I'm not having a cat in the house,' replied Molly.

'Mrs Gymble knows just the cat,' I said. 'A well behaved cat, a paragon of cats. I'm sure you'd love it, once you got to know it.'

137

'I don't like cats. I won't have a cat in my house. You can have what you like outside, but not in the house.'

'But Mrs Gymble says—' I began rather lamely, my hopes receding.

'So you've been making arrangements with Mrs Gymble have you? Behind my back too. Well, you can tell Mrs Gymble I won't have it! Not in the house, anyway.'

'I like that. You're a fine one to talk about going behind your back. What about the geese?'

'What about the geese? Fancy bringing that up. Have the cat if you like, but don't bring it into the house. No. If it's a house cat it'll come sneaking in. If it comes here, I'll get Colonel to drown it.'

'I like cats.'

'Well, I don't.'

'I've always thought there was something the matter with people who didn't like cats.'

'Oh, that's it now. There's something the matter with me. Well, I've always thought that there was something wrong with people who didn't like geese—and now I know there is!'

'You've got the geese, although I don't like them.'

'Yes, but they don't come in the house thieving food; jumping up on the table whenever you turn your back.'

The pigs were making such a commotion when I fed them, squealing, fighting, jumping up at the doors, their mouths slobbering and bubbling with saliva, that I didn't notice Josh Matthews, until he spoke. 'I never did like pigs,' said Josh, his voice raised, 'they do yut too much. An' all out of the bag. Never liked 'em, they do yut too much.'

Josh was a swarthy little man. He had a small farm near The Queen's Head, and kept about a dozen milking cows and a few sheep. Usually he had some store cattle running about,

138

but he didn't fatten them or keep them for long. Josh loved buying and selling, 'havin' a deal', as he said. He attended all the local markets; often his two sons had to milk the cows when they came home from school. When Josh went to market there was no telling what time he'd get back, or in what state. 'Josh was market peart again', it was often said. 'Peart' meaning drunk, and 'market peart', usually meant more drunk than 'peart'.

On days when there were no markets, Josh would, after a cursory spell of work on his farm, tour the locality, calling here and there, hoping to find something to buy or someone to whom he could sell. 'I'm allus willin' to have a go. I'll buy or sell anythin' if I can see a bob or two in it. I'd sell me grandmother if I could make a few bob,' said Josh, his wicked little black eyes dancing. 'But I won't touch pigs, they do yut too much. If you be stuck with 'em, it's grub out o' the bag all the time. With cattle and sheep it's different. I don't mind buyin' old layin' 'ens, that's different, I allus got a 'ome for them. But it ain't the same as 'twas durin' the war an' just after, you could sell anythin' then and get your own price. Scabby ol' apples or anythin'. Folk do keep grumblin' 'bout the government and rationin', but I don't, I 'ope it goes on forever. Yer missus want any sugar? I've got 'old of some, mind the price is well over the odds as you'd expect.'

Josh also had a fund of gossip, some of which was true and a lot that wasn't. It was Josh who told us that Bill Lugg had finally met Olive Cox. ''E's tuppence short, an' so's old Olive. I should think they'll make a good pair if they ever do get wed. But Bill's a good ol' stick. P'rhaps I'll be able to sell 'em a bit of furniture.' More gossip followed and all the time those wicked little black eyes of his were darting about. Josh never missed a thing.

'Let me know if you ever want any cattle or sheep any time,' said Josh, suddenly taking his leave.

'Yes, I will,' I replied, but thought it unlikely. Josh wasn't the man I'd want to buy cattle or sheep from.

We were well into November and fighting a battle against a rising tide of mud. Mud in the fields, deep mud in and around the gateway the cows used, mud in the yard. I fought skirmishes in that yard, scraping its cobbles clean, but soon the mud returned, on the hooves of the cows, on the wheels of tractor and trailer. I fixed a mud scraper by the back door of the house and old sacks lay by the doorway. I took to wearing gumboots all day and every day and took them off before I entered the house.

Everyone now wore gumboots on farms throughout the winter and yet only a few years ago they were only worn on the wettest of days. It was one of those changes that went unnoticed, unremarked. There is a technique to walking in thick mud, the trick is to walk with legs slightly apart to prevent the mud working up. Mud is terrible, in a wet winter it gets into the very soul. Our lives are conditioned and our characters moulded by mud.

A hard frost brought some relief.

It was Sunday morning and the frost had brought the last of the leaves off the ash trees in the rickyard. Cascades of leaves were tumbling and fluttering from the elm trees. From the rickyard I could see the woodland on the hill, the sun shone on its turning leaves; golden, orange, bright yellow, russet mingled with the dark green of the occasional yew tree; looking like Donegal tweed canopying the hillside. This was before the Forestry Commission took it over and laid the hill bare and today there are orderly ranks of dull conifers.

Leaves rustled beneath my feet as I walked, a damp, earthy smell rising from the decaying ones underneath. Brown and silver willow leaves floated on the pond in front of me.

'Hullo,' said a voice behind me. I turned and saw Jack Musgrove in the road, leaning over the crossbar of his bicycle. 'I thought I'd ride over and see what sort of a place you'd got here.' He cocked his head up at the elm trees and then at the barn, studied the falling leaves and said, 'Those leaves'll choke the gutters, you'll want to watch that.'

I took him round the buildings, he inspected every shed; opening doors, walking in, or just peering inside; his head going from left to right, up and down. 'Everything's handy here,' he said. 'Yes, everything's handy, all up together, not much walking from one place to another.'

'Come and see the wheat,' I said. 'And the cows.'

'Nice little plantation,' he remarked when we were in the orchard, the plum tree leaves all drooping, lemon coloured.

'There's quite a lot of gaps down the far end. I know where I can get some plum stocks, I'll plant it up', I said, adding, 'sometime during the winter, when there's a bit of open weather.'

'Oh, I don't know about that,' replied Jack. 'When we planted that little orchard at Suttridge just before the war, it was so cold that the iron bar we were using to make the stake holes stuck to our hands and the ground was frozen hard. "It's no weather to plant trees," I said to the boss. "Pooh," he said, "I've got 'em here and I'm puttin' 'em in. I ain't havin' 'em hangin' about, a bit of frost wun't hurt 'em." Nor it didn't. Every one grew.'

'Goin' to let that hedge go up?' he asked, pointing.

'Yes,' and I nodded my head.

'About three years and it'll be nice to lay. I see you've plenty of willow trees to lop for stakes.'

'Come into the house and have a bottle of beer.'

Jack stood in the kitchen, clutching his cap in his hands.

'Please sit down, Mr Musgrove,' said Molly, 'you look uncomfortable standing there.'

Jack did look ill at ease, gauche almost, standing twisting

141

his cap in his large hands. Not at all like the old Jack I knew and liked so well—I'd rarely seen Jack bareheaded before and he seemed a stranger without his cap. He sat down a yard away from the table, so that he had to stretch his arm out each time he picked up or put down his glass of beer. He seemed shy and hesitant, it was difficult to make conversation at first, but after Molly had been chatting to him for a few minutes he began to talk more easily. A slow smile crept over his face as he remarked, 'By gum—your dinner do smell good,' then with a mischievous glance at Molly, 'I warned him to look out for one as could cook.'

'How are things at Suttridge?' I asked.

'We've got all the wheat in and we've finished the mangolds, my back's only just recovered from throwing them in that old barn. You know. You've had some of it.' Jack gave me a faint smile and sipped his beer. 'And the boss is thinking about buying a new tractor. Oh—and we had a bullock die. When the boss found him dead, about eight o'clock in the morning, he came to me and said, "That mottle-faced bullock's dead. I wouldn't have had that happen for fifty pound." And after he'd had his breakfast he came out and said to me, "I wouldn't have had that happen for sixty pound." About eleven o'clock, he said, "You know, Jack, that bullock was worth eighty quid." And after the knacker had taken it away, he said, "That bullock was worth over a hundred quid—and now I'll be lucky if I get three for it." When he came out in the afternoon, I thought to myself, that bullock's goin' to be worth a hundred and twenty now, but he never mentioned it no more.'

'How's Walter getting on, working for Mr Barnard?' asked Molly.

'Well,' said Jack slowly, 'you do know old Walt, proper old stick in the mud, he is. Every time I do see him, he says "Barnard ain't a farmer like Clutterbuck, he'll never grow maltin' samples of barley like Clutterbuck, 'e don't believe in muck like Clutterbuck, 'e's all for the bag stuff." That's what old Walt do keep sayin'. An' he wun't learn to drive the tractor, I told'n that wasn't no good, 'e'd 'ave to keep up with the times. But there, you've worked alongside old Walt, you do know what 'e is, stubborn as an old mule, a good chap and all that, but he've got his little ways, as you're bound to know.' Jack smiled at Molly. 'But he'll come to in time,' he said.

Jack suddenly started chuckling and looking at me, said, 'D'you remember the time when the rat ran up old Walt's trouser leg at dreshin'? I said to 'im after, "Walt," I said, "if thee 'adn't caught this rat when thee did, your missus 'ould 'ave to 'ave taken a lodger in."' Jack suddenly stopped chuckling and looked confused, regretting his remark, until he noticed that Molly was laughing.

'Did you know that Bill is courting?' I asked.

'Oh yes, I've seen her. A fat old boiling piece.' Jack grinned and added, 'Old Bill wun't ever get married. 'E ain't the sort.'

After twiddling with his cap for a few minutes, he said, 'My son's leavin' school at Christmas. He's goin' in for engineerin', he don't want farmwork, not at any price. You can't blame him, the work's hard and the pay's low.' Jack paused before saying, 'If he'd have been interested in farmin' I might have tried to have got a little place that we could have worked together. I've got a few bob put by, but as 'tis I shan't bother, I'm quite content with me otchards, and working for the boss.' He drained his glass and I offered him another, but he said, 'I shall have to be off, the missus will be wonderin' where I've got to.'

'In a couple of years', Jack said, catching hold of the handlebars of his bicycle, 'I'll come and lay that hedge. Have a few days of me holidays. I could make a nobby job of that, right by the road. That would give people somethin' to look at, that would. That is, if you'd like me to.'

143

'I'd be delighted if you would.'

He cocked a leg over his bicycle. 'Well, so long,' he said, and pedalled away.

Soon all the trees were bare of leaf. I went into the orchard and saw that every yellowing leaf, so recently hanging prettily and gracefully from the plum trees, had fallen, making the orchard look suddenly stark, with its rows of trees, straight from whichever angle they were viewed. Ever since, winter has begun for me on the day the orchard is suddenly leafless.

A drying wind and a few slight frosts dried the ground a little. November became December; the tracery of the bare trees against the grey winter sky, old December's bareness everywhere. But I hadn't time to stand and stare. I could hear the familiar groan of Owen's lorry coming to take two lots of weaner pigs to market.

The pig trade was up, mine sold well, making the highest price for weaners in the market. I gave the buyer the customary luck money, which he spat on—not in contempt, but for additional luck—before pocketing it. Mr Bishop was busy selling store sheep, but later he said to me, 'I hear you had some good weaners today and they topped the market. You ought to think about having some sheep.'

I had thought about sheep, but seeing the hollow bottoms of some of my hedges, I'd hesitated. Perhaps next year I'd buy a few ewes at one of the autumn sheep sales. 'A few store lambs would get as fat as butter on your land,' said Mr Bishop, as he hurried away.

CHAPTER THIRTEEN

Supper with the Darcys

The week before Christmas the weather turned cold. The cows picked their way through the mud; hard and frozen, the sharp edges cut their feet. They congregated by the gateway even earlier in the afternoon, waiting for the food in the mangers and racks.

When I'd finished all the routine work on the morning of Christmas Eve I went to gather some ivy, holly and mistletoe. Molly was busy in the kitchen making mince pies. It was a cold, still morning; there'd been a sharp frost during the night, the short grass in the orchard was crisp and furry and crunched beneath my feet. The sun in the grey sky shone hesitantly above the stiff branches of the bare elm

145

trees, and the frost glistened on the lichen encrusted apple boughs from which I cut the mistletoe.

The scarlet berries of holly in the hedgerow gave this austere world of grey skies, black trees and white frost a welcome touch of colour. And so did the orange beak of the blackbird who watched me cut the holly. With head cocked, alert and apprehensive, he regarded me with a baleful eye. 'That's my food, that's my food', he seemed to be saying, beak aslant, accusingly. I felt guilty, plundering the handsome bird's larder and felt obliged to murmur, 'I'm only taking a few sprigs, there's plenty left.' At the sound of my voice, or perhaps at my assurance, he hopped away, saying I like to fancy, 'That's all right then.'

I pulled some ivy from the crumbling garden wall, disturbing a pair of wood pigeons feasting on the berries. I didn't feel in the least guilty about robbing them, they had and would rob me of more than enough.

When I returned, Molly was sweeping the flagstones outside the kitchen window. 'You haven't brought much holly,' she said, still busy with her sweeping.

'No, you see there was this blackbird ...' I started to explain, but the turbulent arrival of Mrs Gymble on her bicycle interrupted me.

'Here are the sprouts,' she puffed, thrusting a basket at Molly. 'Fred says they're a present.'

Molly started to thank her, but Mrs Gymble, eyeing the ivy, holly and mistletoe, said, 'Don't you get putting that up 'til after mid-day, 'tis unlucky, or so they do say. I like a bit of holly and mistletoe in the house at Christmastide, but what I really likes is them paper chains and big paper balls and a few balloons—ever so jolly, I always think. You got paper decorations to put up?'

Molly shook her head.

'No, well you'll have to have 'em when you got kids, and a tree with baubles. Mine love it, an' my Fred do—he's every bit as bad as the kids. "Fred," I says to him, "You're nothing but a great kid yourself." But it's nice, isn't it? I likes to see everybody happy and jolly, especially at Christmas, and it's kids, I always say, what makes Christmas. You wants to get and think about it soon, get and fill this great house up.'

'Yes,' said Molly, as she took Mrs Gymble into the kitchen, 'we'll have children, all in good time, just give us time to get settled down. I'll have a boy first, I hope.'

'I always says it don't matter whether it's a boy or a girl as long as it's sound and healthy. Course, farmers always want sons to carry on the farm. 'Tis natural like, but you be thankful for what the good Lord do send you, if it's strong and healthy.'

'Mind,' said Mrs Gymble when she was seated, 'I'm glad when the time comes to take 'em down.' Molly looked startled. I was bound to say, 'Take them down where?' 'So's I can give the place a good clean,' explained Mrs Gymble, 'The kids say leave 'em up a bit longer, and Fred, he'd weaken, but I says no, down they come. 'Tis unlucky to leave 'em up after twelfth night, anyway.'

Mrs Gymble took a workman-like bite at a mince pie. Molly overfilled her mince pies with mincemeat and as Mrs Gymble's teeth closed the pie burst and hot mincemeat oozed over her chin and trickled down her neck. 'Fierce little chaps,' exclaimed Mrs Gymble, hastily dabbing with a handkerchief. Molly's mince pies, I'd learnt, needed to be treated with caution—not that I'd said so, since the tripe episode I'd been careful with comments about her cooking.

'Fred'll be bringing you some roses once this frost's gone,' said Mrs Gymble, as she was leaving. 'He growed them hisself from cuttings, so they won't have suckers like them you buys from a nursery, he told me to tell you.'

On Christmas morning the lorry driver came much earlier

than usual to collect our milk, in a hurry to finish work and return to his family. The postman was late and in no hurry. He came into the house and had a drink—he looked as though he'd had several already—and a mince pie.

'Them pies be proper morish,' he said, smacking his lips. He became loquacious, recalling earlier Christmasses, people long since dead. 'Ah, that was the year old Brown had all—no, no 'twasn't, that were another time, and now I think on't, 'tweren't Brown at all—' His memories were all confused, but he found them no less amusing for that. Two drinks and three mince pies later—I don't know whose was the greater pleasure, his in eating or Molly's in giving—he slung his bag over his shoulder and said he must be on his way. 'But before I go', he announced roguishly, 'I'll give 'e a song.'

'Christmas comes but once a year, but once a year,
    And it's everybody's job to keep it up, to keep it up—'
At the word 'up' he raised his right knee quickly.

Soon after the postman's departure Uncle George came, bearing several bottles of his home made wine and a box of chocolates for Molly. He had to look in the oven and inspect the cockerel he'd given us, but he didn't stop long.

'I'd like to stop,' he said, and obviously meant it. 'I'd like to stop and have some of that bird—damn my rags, ain't he a good 'un, I picked out the best for you—but you know 'ow 'tis. I allus go to me brother's, an' Ethel 'ould be that upset if I didn't. I'd aim as 'er'd be cut to the quick if I missed a year. An' Boxin' Day I allus goes to Aggie's, she do make me very welcome. But there ain't much pleasure sat at the table facing that Sam Fisher. He don't speak or anythin', just guzzle an' guts an' break wind—no manners. You'd think he'd speak an' try to be civil. I'd sooner sit with a Chinaman, at least he'd smile, even if you couldn't understand what he was sayin'.'

On Boxing Day we went to my parents.

'I thought our George was coming,' said Father as we sat down to cold turkey.

'You know, Father, that he's gone to Aggie's,' replied Mother, adding, 'though how he'll fare there, I don't know. That Aggie never was much of a cook, not to my way of thinking.'

'She used to make some lovely rice pudding when she was a girl, with good thick skins on 'em.'

'Oh. Well, you can't live on rice puddings. Not day after day.'

'Not day after day, Ethel. I agree with you.'

'Anyway, rice puddings aren't the thing for Christmas. We're having another of my Christmas puddings.'

'Our George didn't half enjoy that one yesterday.'

Mother turned to Molly. 'What sort of a day did you two have? Very quiet on your own in that great farmhouse. You should have come here. And what was your Christmas pudding like? You should have let me make your puddings.'

'I thought for sure our George was coming,' mumbled Father.

After we had eaten, we sat round the fire and talked. Then we had to leave and hurry home to do the milking and feed the stock.

A few days after Christmas, the trees and hedges were festooned with thick hoar frost. The rime hung white and heavy from the branches making the trees stiff and the air still. It was ear tingling, finger biting weather. You didn't stand about unless you had to, you soon began to stamp your feet. Everything seemed hushed, even the foot stamping produced only muffled thuds. And so I was even more surprised to see old Mr Darcy walking towards our house.

He came inside our yard, well buttoned against the cold, a cap pulled down over his ears, thick woollen gloves on his hands; hands that he kept beating against his sides.

'Hullo, Mr Darcy,' I called. 'Whatever brings you over here today? Come inside.'

'My sisters sent me to ask you both if you will come for supper and to spend the evening with us tomorrow.'

'No, no,' he said, when I had got him inside the kitchen and by the fire. 'I won't take off my coat, I'll just unbutton it. I must be getting back, my sisters will want to know. I should have come yesterday, but I didn't feel up to it. No, no,' waving his hand at me as I was about to speak, 'I'm perfectly well today. And my sisters said, "Charles, you must go this morning." And here I am.'

'Mr Darcy and his sisters have invited us to supper tomorrow,' I told Molly. Molly thanked him and said, 'It's such a cold morning, you shouldn't be out at all you know. Let me give you a hot drink before you go back.'

But Mr Darcy refused a drink and started to button up his overcoat; right up tight to the neck, his chin poking over the top of the velvet collar. 'I've quite got my breath back. I must be going.' Tugging his woollen gloves on, 'My sisters will want to know.'

At the doorway he paused and, pulling his cap well down, added, 'Seven tomorrow then. Agatha is very particular about time.' I walked across the yard with him and watched him potter along the road; his legs taking short steps and his head well forward.

'We must set off in good time,' said Molly, the following evening. 'You know how fussy Miss Agatha is about time.'

Their house was almost a mile away. The stars were shining brightly, and as we walked along the rough road through the fields our feet crunched on the frozen surface.

Miss Agatha and Miss Harriet met us at the door. Miss Agatha with her hair dressed in a bun high on her head and Miss Harriet's in coils over her ears, both of them wearing ankle length dresses of decidedly late Victorian fashion. After taking our coats they showed us into the living room and Mr Darcy came with outstretched hand to welcome us.

It was like stepping back fifty years to step inside that room. The oil lamp gave a soft glow to the solid Victorian furniture. A dining table with bulbous legs was covered by a stiff white cloth on which was now displayed glinting silver and sparkling glass; a sideboard with an extravagantly carved back; a glass fronted bookcase and chairs with upholstered seats and backs, all in mahogany. In the far corner stood a harmonium and a round music stool, and under a window a rosewood bureau. The windows were draped with dark red tasselled chenille curtains.

Around the inglenook fireplace were comfortable easy chairs, deeply buttoned and again upholstered in rich red velvet. 'Please do sit down,' said Miss Harriet, indicating these chairs, and when we were seated, Miss Agatha spoke, 'Will you take a glass of sherry wine?'

Logs burned merrily in the fire basket; apple and pear logs which gave off a pleasant aroma. I half expected Mr Pickwick to enter and sit beside us, stretching his legs toward the fire and exclaiming, 'This is indeed comfort.' But glancing at Mr Darcy, glass in hand, the firelight flickering on his face, rosy from the fire's glow, I thought, perhaps he's already here.

Miss Agatha put her glass on a small round table, covered with a dark green chenille cloth. She rested her hands in her lap and said, 'It's so nice to be neighbourly.'

'That's Father,' said Miss Harriet, pointing to a large framed photograph on the wall of a stern faced, mutton-chopped gentleman. 'And next to him is Mother.' She too, wore a forbidding expression. 'And over there by the sideboard is Great Uncle Jack and Great Aunt Harriet—and over there is Grandfather Darcy with Uncle Herbert on his left.' I looked at each of them in turn and, so it seemed, they gazed solemnly back at me.

'Every Boxing Day, we used to have our neighbours in,' said Miss Agatha. 'That was years ago when Mother and Father were here. Harriet and I were busy helping Mother all day with the preparations. And after supper Mother would play the harmonium and Father would sing—he had a fine baritone voice. Some of the other gentlemen would join in.' Miss Agatha sighed and added, 'We had such jollifications in the days when we were young.'

'There doesn't seem to be the neighbourliness today,' said Mr Darcy. 'We were so pleased when we heard you were coming to Perrygrove,' put in Miss Harriet.

'And Harvest Suppers,' said Miss Agatha. 'Mother and Harriet and I, and the maidservants—we had servants in those days—we used to wait on the men. Father at the head of the table, carving from a huge joint of beef.'

'We never went out much. We didn't need to,' explained Miss Harriet.

'All the old ways and customs seem to be dying out,' sighed Miss Agatha. 'We don't get any carol singers now. I used to enjoy them. We'd invite them in for a glass of something and a mince pie. But the wassaillers still come, though they've not been this year yet. They haven't been to you, have they?' She looked up sharply, fearful lest they'd been missed this year.

'No,' I reassured her.

'I expect it's a bit early yet. They always come to us.'

Miss Agatha placed another log on the fire. 'That man Biggs, goes by the name of Colonel, promised to come and saw some logs for us,' she said, 'but he never came. Charles had to saw them himself, and do you know, that after a morning of it he was bathered right out.'

152

'I never had much opinion of that man Biggs,' said Mr Darcy.

We seated ourselves at the table and Mr Darcy said grace. '—*may the Lord make us truly grateful. Amen.*' Heads looked up, bobbed up rather, there were little smiles on the faces of brother and sisters.

Miss Agatha carved the ham. 'Charles doesn't like carving,' she explained. Miss Harriet passed a dish of steaming mashed potatoes and Mr Darcy offered us pickled walnuts, various home made chutneys and pickles. The ham was followed by trifle, topped with whipped cream. 'We used to make all our own butter and cheese in days gone by,' said Miss Agatha, wistfully.

'And bake our own bread. We kept the flour in a large wooden bin. And cured our own hams and bacon,' said Miss Harriet.

'I want to start baking my own bread,' said Molly. 'And we've got a pig to kill in a week or so.'

'Ah, that's what I like to hear. You can't beat home produced victuals,' said Mr Darcy, 'I never had much opinion of this mass produced stuff.'

When we were once more seated round the fireplace, Miss Agatha said, 'The farm had got too much for Charles, it used to worry him so. He was never very strong. And what with the difficulty of getting suitable labour and the regulations and restrictions and all those dreadful forms and officials banging on the door and plaguing us, we decided to give up. Charles wasn't getting any younger and his chest was getting worse. And then, when our best worker retired, we could never find anyone suitable to replace him.'

'We were offered a good price for the farm', continued Miss Agatha, 'so we decided to sell. On condition that we remained in the house, we wouldn't have liked moving, not at our time of life. And we kept an orchard and Charles kept his favourite cow. He milks her himself, he likes to do that. I don't know how long he'll be able to, he hasn't got the best of health, but he loves that cow, spends hours fussing and talking to her. In the summer he goes into the orchard and sits on her back, she's that quiet.'

'I went into the museum in Westgate Street,' Mr Darcy said. 'I remember seeing most of the tools in the farming room being used, some I've used myself. I even met a man once who'd used a breast plough, killing work he said that was. A good man could mow an acre a day with a scythe. Father used to dibble horse beans in; the men with the dibbers going across the fields making holes and the women and boys coming behind popping the beans in. They don't seem able to grow beans these days. Four of oats to one of beans, that was wonderful feed for milk. We grew all our own food for the animals. This cube stuff they buy today, goodness knows what's in it.'

'Some folks used to put colouring in their butter,' said Miss Harriet, 'but we never did. We didn't need to.'

'We were up at half past five every morning,' put in Miss Agatha, 'and busy all day long, although we had maids. Busy with the butter and the cheese and the poultry, as well as the housework. Then, of course, there was our needlework. But we liked it, we were happy, we wouldn't have changed, not for anything. And Father was always good to his workmen, and Charles was too. That makes a difference.'

'Father used to reckon it was a poor crop if he didn't grow well over fifty bushels of wheat to the acre. And that was without artificials. Of course, we used to have great steaming dung heaps, you don't see many of them today,' said Mr Darcy.

'Charles was always so tender hearted,' said Miss Agatha. 'It used to upset him when we had to sell an old cow.'

Mr Darcy rose and went over to the glass-fronted bookcase. He extracted two leather bound volumes and handed them to me. Miss Harriet was telling Molly that she

154

knitted her brother's socks, he wouldn't have socks from a shop. The books were about farming in Gloucestershire and were published in the eighteenth century. As I fingered the stiff leaves, Mr Darcy continued talking.

Miss Agatha and Miss Harriet were both talking to Molly, both at the same time and both about different things. Molly was sitting between the sisters, turning her head to left and right in quick succession. Not much conversation was expected of her—she was only able to put a word in here and there. A little later, while Mr Darcy was quietly telling me about the farming of his youth, I overheard the sisters ask Molly about her house, garden and poultry. I had an opportunity to observe the two sisters as Mr Darcy made many long pauses, gazing dreamily into the fire.

Both sisters now listened attentively to Molly, bobbing their heads occasionally and smiling at each other and then at Molly, in approbation of what she said.

'Such a big house,' said Miss Agatha at one point. 'You must have to be busy.'

'We haven't got many rooms furnished.'

'No, of course not,' said Miss Agatha. 'But we might be able to find you a few bits, we'd let you have them very reasonable.'

'We've far too much,' whispered Miss Harriet, 'We used to go to sales and couldn't resist buying a nice piece of furniture being sold at a reasonable price.'

'I never had much opinion of Bramleys,' said Mr Darcy, returning from his fire gazing reverie, 'I've always thought Newtons were a better apple.'

'I'm told you're doing such good work in your garden,' said Miss Agatha.

As Molly spoke of lavender, jasmine, honeysuckle, thyme, pinks, columbines, and hollyhocks, the sisters bobbed their heads, smiled approvingly and made exclamations of delight.

'Lavender,' said one, 'jasmine,' said the other. But when Miss Agatha told Molly she must have dahlias, Mr Darcy commented, 'I never had any opinion of dahlias—earwigs.'

'Take no notice of Charles, he always says that,' said Miss Agatha. 'We'll see if we can find you some plants.'

'At the right time,' whispered Miss Harriet.

'Of course it'll be at the right time, Harriet,' said Miss Agatha rather sharply. 'She knows that, she's a sensible girl, so different from most of the girls today who seem to be such flipperty gibbets.'

When Molly told them she intended to fatten cockerels for sale next Christmas, they advised her to get Light Sussex cockerels.

Molly was telling them that as soon as we could afford it she'd like to get some of the rooms decorated—at the moment most of the rooms were papered and painted in depressing shades of brown.

'We know the very man,' said Miss Agatha.

'And so reasonable, we always find,' added Miss Harriet.

'I want the kitchen, the hall, and passages done in white,' said Molly, warming to her theme. And as she said this, the sisters kept muttering, 'Well well. In white. Well, well.'

I think Miss Agatha and Miss Harriet would have continued discussing our house and garden with Molly for some time. But Mr Darcy was quietly dropping off to sleep, his eyelids were drooping and his head nodding. 'Shrub roses,' Molly was saying, her face slightly flushed with pleasure at the old ladies' interest. 'Musk roses, moss roses,' said Miss Agatha, 'you must have musk roses and moss roses.'

'It's been a delightful evening, but we really must be leaving,' I said.

'You must take a drop of ginger wine before you leave', insisted Miss Agatha, 'to warm you. Harriet, pour some wine at once. Charles, Charles, rouse yourself, our guests are leaving.'

All three stood in the doorway to wish us goodbye. 'Please come again,' said Miss Agatha, 'it's been a real pleasure to have someone who's interested in the old ways and times.'

We left the elderly trio framed in the doorway, the sisters waving, their brother holding a hurricane lantern. 'Goodbye,' we called across the courtyard, a warm shaft from the lantern lighting our way.

CHAPTER FOURTEEN

The common task, the daily round

On New Year's Day Molly's parents came to stay for a few days. Her father was tall, slim, very upright, bespectacled and with hair slightly greying at the temples; in repose he had a stern appearance which vanished when a shy smile slowly spread over his face, as it frequently did. He was the headmaster of a school in Bristol. His wife was a few years younger, of medium height and inclined to be plump, a gay laughing person, with very black hair and vivacious eyes.

They were rather bemused by our country life and ways; it was obvious that they had some romantic vision of country and farming life, some vague idea of A Merrie England, of dancing on the village green and rosy-cheeked milkmaids carrying milk in wooden pails. Farmers were either jolly red-faced gentlemen or gnarled, irascible, and perhaps cunning, old peasants.

They were surprised and disappointed not to find the dairy arrayed with setting pans of milk for cream and butter, butter churns and cheese presses. They couldn't understand why we didn't make butter and cheese. 'But with all this milk, ' they exclaimed, 'and you say you can buy it cheaper, how peculiar,' and looked perplexed.

'Surely,' said Molly's father in a schoolmasterly fashion, 'it would pay you to retail your own milk instead of sending it away in churns. You should consider things like that, you know.'

Molly explained that we hadn't the time, to which he replied, 'Surely you could sell some at the door?'

He listened carefully while we spoke of retail licences and the Milk Marketing Board, was surprised that grass just didn't grow willy nilly, and that food for cows actually cost money. He didn't like the idea of artificial insemination, and thought we'd have had some fine stamping bull. Molly's mother, on the other hand, was relieved to hear that we had no bull. Visions of her daughter being gored by such an animal must have worried her ever since Molly had joined the Land Army.

Over all this and much else, my father-in-law gravely nodded or shook his head; a most courteous man, he refrained from making any adverse comments, but I felt his worst suspicions about farming and farming ways were being confirmed.

My in-laws had expected to find horses in the stable; father-in-law must have been reading about horses, he kept discoursing about the relative merits of Shires and Clydesdales. I began to think we'd let the couple down. Mother-in-law kept repeating, 'This big house, this big house, I don't know how poor Moll manages. And all that mud.'

159

The mud was a shock to Father-in-law too. He'd come, as he thought, suitably clothed to accompany us about the farm, but soon found his country clothes and boots inadequate in our mud.

Both fell in love with the calves and vowed they'd never eat veal again, and were surprised that animals were bred and kept especially for beef; all beef they'd supposed, was from cows no longer wanted for milking. They fussed over our bacon pig in the cot, too fat now to be anything but docile; they liked giving him scraps of food, scratching his back and listening to his good humoured grunts. 'He's so friendly. How can you kill and eat him?' they asked. I didn't answer, I'd begun to wonder that myself.

'Ah, cider,' said Father-in-law on the first night, when they were seated in front of our big open fireplace. 'I've always wanted to sit round an inglenook fireplace, with the sight of burning logs and the smell of wood smoke, quaffing farmhouse cider.'

He pronounced the cider 'palatable', and drank several mugfuls, despite my warnings; like many townspeople he supposed it to be an innocuous drink. Towards bedtime he became quite merry and sang a verse or two of *The Farmer's Boy*. As he made his way up our wide oaken stairway, he was rather tottery and clutched the bannister. At breakfast next morning he said very slowly, 'That cider's some pretty powerful stuff,' and during the remainder of his visit his drinking was more moderate.

They both thought our life a spartan one; cold water for washing; the constant water pumping, the regular cold draught that blew and whistled through the house, the frost and ice that formed on the bedroom window panes, the early rising to milk the cows. The lack of electricity, main water, daily newspapers and transport. But most of all the cold, in the house and outside, the vicious wind that whipped round the buildings.

160

Molly's mother voiced her concern, forgetting that such had been her daughter's life for several years. 'My dear, how do you stand it? Are you sure you won't be ill? I never realised that this was the kind of life you led.'

Molly laughed. 'This isn't the first time you've been to the country, Mother. You visited us when I was with the Clutterbucks.'

'Yes, dear, but it was always in the summer. Do wrap up well. You don't wear warm enough clothes. In those thick breeches one minute and in thin stockings the next. It's a wonder you don't catch your death. Those flimsy knickers you wear may be all right in the summer, but you really should wear some thick woollen ones in the winter in a place like this.'

We accompanied them to the station and saw them off on the train. They'd been delighted to see Molly, but they were equally delighted to be returning to the comforts of town.

'Come again soon,' we shouted, as the train started to steam out. 'In the summer,' they answered as they waved, heads poking from the carriage window, half enveloped in smoke and steam.

Three days later Molly received a parcel by post from her mother. It contained pairs of warm, fleecy bloomers, woollen vests, thick ribbed woollen stockings and two large flanelette nightdresses that a staid Victorian matron would not have disdained. 'I won't wear them!' said Molly.

All the water for the house, for washing the milking utensils and for cooling the milk, had to be pumped by hand into an overhead storage tank. It was anguishing to see all that water, so laboriously pumped, running away after it had been through the cooler. That hand pumping was a twice daily task. After every milking I stationed myself at the semi-rotary pump, and pumped and pumped. Oh, how well

I came to know the feel of that pump handle, the backwards and forwards motion; the sound of the pump and of the water splashing into the tank above. I can feel that handle now, my arm going to and fro. I can still hear those old familiar sounds, the clank of the pump and the sound of splashing water. And as I write, my ears as in a dream, I strain to catch the first sound of water from the overflow pipe. That's what we listened for as we pumped, the sound of water from the overflow, and we counted the strokes; four hundred, or was it five hundred before we could expect that welcome sound from the overflow pipe?

It was a job that could never be missed, or even put off. How tempting to have breakfast first, especially with the smell of it so close. Yes, how tempting to leave the pumping until after breakfast—and how fatal. How frustrating to be pumping, fifty, fifty-one, fifty-two, when there was work to be done in the fields. When I had urgent work Molly sometimes did the pumping. Are you sure you filled the tank to overflowing? Did you count backwards and forwards? Have you left a tap dripping? These were some of the eternal questions we asked each other.

Water is a precious commodity, and when you've had to pump your supply by hand you value it. And yet, how it is squandered. If everyone had to pump their entire supply of water for twelve months it would be a lesson never forgotten. Even now I cannot bear to see a tap left running, or even a dripping tap, or water used wastefully. I remember those years of twice daily pumping.

Another twice daily task, for half of the year, was the lighting of lanterns. Not the ordinary hurricane lanterns which gave only a poor light, but the Tilley lanterns which we used for house and cowshed. It was all a matter of patience and method with these lanterns which, when lit, gave a good light. The jets had to be clean, mantles in good condition, (with replacements to hand), and we had to have a supply of methylated spirit as well as lamp burning oil. It was so easy to run out of methylated spirit, but without it the lamps could not be lit. The clip-on lighters were soaked in meths first then clipped under the mantle and lit, and this caused the oil in the lantern to vapourise, (the lanterns had built in pressure pumps). If we tried to hurry the vapourising process, by turning the jets on too quickly—and I invariably did this—the whole process was a failure. Molly was much better at the job than I was so, after my first fumbling efforts, she took charge of this.

The lanterns also gave out quite a heat, accompanied by a continuous hissing. I think the hissing had a soporific effect, and this, together with our open fire—even more soporific, —often had us dozing in our armchairs by eight o'clock on winter evenings.

Perrygrove had been licensed by the Ministry of Agriculture for an attested herd and the production of T. T. milk while Barnard had been the occupier. Even so, they weren't happy about it, but as the building had been passed for Barnard, they couldn't very well refuse them for me. Instead they niggled; various officials called, hummed and hawed and made suggestions.

The Dairy Officer, Miss James, was a frequent visitor. As she clambered out of her small Morris motor car she was apologetic. 'I'm sorry to worry you, my dears, but it's the regulations. And I must, I simply must see that the regulations and requirements are met.'

She was fussy, sometimes a little tiresome, but she was also friendly and helpful. Despite all the fiddly little things she tried to make us do and her occasional bossiness, we soon learnt that she was a kindly warm hearted person. A reproach from her was always softened by a word of praise. She must have been close to sixty; plump and rather short, with grey untidy hair. A cloak would have suited her, but as it was she wore flowing clothes, voluminous skirts.

Stepping into our dairy she exclaimed, 'Wood, wood, you'll have to alter that. We can't have that.' And then, almost in ecstasy she added, 'How lovely to see nice new brushes and gleaming new pails!'

Our cowshed provided her with an apparently endless source of objections. 'Wooden hay racks! The Ministry doesn't like those, but if you creosote them you can keep them. And make some nose holes in the wall so that the cows can breath fresh air.' I creosoted the hay rack and because of the smell had difficulty in getting the cows into the shed. But I didn't make the nose holes. On her next visit, Miss James, eager as a blood-hound made straight for the cowshed. 'You've creosoted the rack, excellent, excellent,' she cried, clapping her hands. I waited for her to remark about the non-existence of nose holes but nothing was said. All her attention was given to the windows which wouldn't open. 'I can't open the windows,' she said. I explained that they hadn't been made to open. 'You must make them open. That's it, make them open. That's the answer, make them open. Next time I come, remember.'

We soon found that Miss James didn't always remember what she'd ordered, she was far too busy thinking of other things for us to do. We also found that the thing to do was to lure her away from shed and dairy as quickly as possible before she found too many 'little jobs that simply must be done'. We found the best way to do that too. Miss James dearly liked a cup of tea or coffee and she was inordinately fond of chocolate cake. Molly made a good chocolate cake and it proved irresistible to Miss James. And Molly took great care always to keep chocolate cake in a tin ready for Miss James.

When Miss James arrived Molly would wait ten minutes and then go to her and say, 'I've just made a pot of tea, Miss James.'

'Oh, lovely, lovely,' Miss James would say, patting her hands together. 'I'd love a cup of tea, my dear.' It was obvious that she was fond of Molly and the two had become firm friends. 'Just what I needed, my dear,' she'd say, sitting down at the kitchen table. 'A slice of cake, Miss James?' Molly would ask.

'Simply delicious, my dear,' said Miss James, as she munched away.

Molly would pour her some more tea and ask, 'Another slice of cake?' 'Oh, I shouldn't,' but Miss James's hand would already be stretching towards it. I mustn't give the impression that Miss James wasn't consciencious, she was, but she could be side-tracked about all those minor 'little jobs'. On the whole she hadn't an easy job. Some milking premises were in a shocking state and some farmers' milking methods were deplorable. She often met with abuse, but that didn't deter her, she returned again and again until some improvement was effected.

We were still waiting for the telephone to be installed when Buttercup's heifer calf was taken ill; it was a still crisp night in January, the moon was bright and a fox was howling when I went to telephone Mr Carmichael. The calf was dead before he arrived; unable to determine the cause of death, he put the calf in the boot of his car so that he could examine it further at his surgery and if necessary send it, or parts of it, to a laboratory in Bristol. Buttercup herself, was doing well, much better than we'd expected, she was still giving over five gallons of milk each day.

A week or ten days later we had a frightening experience with some of the calves that had been born during the early autumn. They had apparently gone mad, they leapt in the air and fell about, their bodies contorted, their heads twisted underneath them. Their sweating bodies were racked by violent convulsions, it seemed as if they would kill themselves before the vet had seen them. But, unbelievably, they survived until his arrival. He immediately diagnosed lead poisoning and drenched them with Epsom salts which neutralised the lead. We found a small spot on the door of the shed which the calves had been licking. Andrew Carmichael scraped at the door with a pocket knife and underneath a layer of tar discovered paint. 'There's your trouble,' he said, scraping some flakes of dried paint into a tin which he put into his pocket. 'I'll examine it, but I'm sure that's the cause. There've probably been calves in here for years and never any trouble. It often happens like that.'

We saw a lot of Andrew Carmichael and his assistants. Our animals, particularly the cattle, were smitten with all kinds of illness, familiar and unfamiliar; some were mysterious, never explained, like the death of Buttercup's calf. It was not an unusual experience Andrew Carmichael assured me; it happened to many new farmers, and to experienced farmers moving to a fresh farm. After a couple of years the troubles usually ceased, possibly because the herd became acclimatised to the surroundings and an immunity built up. It was, said Carmichael, the hardest job to keep a new client for the first two years; faced with a sea of apparently never ending trouble, the farmer lost confidence in the vet and went to another. Barnard was adamant that his animals had never been afflicted with most of the troubles that beset mine; his stock had never suffered from the various deficiency diseases which drove me almost to despair.

One of Andrew Carmichael's favourite remedies was strong black coffee; I must have poured gallons of it down animals' throats. Well, not exactly poured. Drenching had to be done with care, it was easy enough to choke an animal. I became adept at drenching cows, not only with coffee but with a variety of medicants; grasping the animal's nose with fingers and thumb and with the other hand thrusting a long

necked bottle into the animal's mouth and gently tipping the
liquid down its throat.

Andrew Carmichael was fond of coffee; when in relaxed
mood he would come into the house, sit down in our kitchen
and drink cup after cup of coffee and eat all the biscuits in
Molly's tin. Sometimes he would recite Robert Burns;
Scottish like so many vets, his accent was hardly discernible,
but when reciting Burns it became thick and rich. After a
few verses of Burns he would become expansive and
reminisce about his various experiences.

That was one side of him; he could be abrupt, taciturn
and impatient. No doubt his moods were due to the pressure
of work, late night calls, and heavy, difficult cases. On these
days he would start hooting on the horn of his motor long
before he reached Perrygrove. Hoot, hoot, hoot, as he drove
into our yard with a rush of wheels, a screech of brakes;
prolonged hooting before he got out and closed the door.

Carmichael wasn't so bad, he didn't make a fettish of it,
but on arrival his assistants went through the ritual of
'togging-up'. One shoe off, one wader on; second shoe off,
second wader on; jacket taken off and stowed in boot of car,
rubberised smock taken from boot, donned and fastened at
back, while I waited ready with water, soap, towel or
whatever needed. Then began the clump, clump, clump,
towards the sick animal. What with the clumping, the
flapping, the sloshing and rustling of their apparel, the smell
of disinfectant and medicine; it was no wonder that the poor
animals were sometimes startled out of their wits. 'Is she
wild?' they'd ask. 'Not usually,' I would reply, cautiously;
but you never could be sure, not even with the most docile
animal when suddenly confronted with such an apparition.

The milking machine was installed, a two bucket unit, the
vacuum pump driven by a small petrol engine. It lightened

and speeded up the milking, but what with the cattle and pigs to be attended to, ditches to be dug and various other jobs to be done and the prospect of spring planting, I was looking for help, if only for a few days a week.

The milking, the feeding of stock; cleaning the cowshed and washing the milking machine and utensils, they all took time and bit into the day. Then there was the littering of stock, cleaning out the pigsties; all these were regular, daily or twice daily jobs; and there was too, of course, the pumping of water.

We were also getting short of money; the pig and cattle food from the Farmers' Stores, the sum we had to pay arising from the valuation, the milking machine and the vet's bills; they had depleted our slender resources. We began to dread the arrival of the postman about halfway through the month with his cargo of bills.

The postman came every weekday morning, even if he hadn't any letters for us. When we had first come to Perrygrove he'd said, 'I'll call every morning, you may have letters to post, and I'll always bring any small thing you may be needing from the village.'

Every morning Molly gave him a cup of tea and while he was drinking it he told us the local news. It was the postman who told us of Caleb Pocock's death.

'Ah', he said, after making his announcement, 'he's gone, he's gone. He hung on as long as he could, but he's gone at last. He were a tight 'un, but I'm sorry he's gone, we wun't see another like 'em. He were a wonderful chap in the garden. Tight mind. D'ya know, when his poor old missus were alive, he used to make 'er pay for the vegetables from the garden. Out of the 'ousekeepin'! Ah well, don't speak ill of the dead I allus say. He were a wonderful chap an' we'll miss 'im, we shall. God bless 'is soul, Amen.'

Caleb's death was no surprise, it was a wonder that he'd clung to life for so long. He'd always been a stubborn, dogged old man, and the trait had persisted to the very last. Jack, Bill, Gritton and I were bearers at his funeral, and his housekeeper wept copiously during the service. Later we learnt that Caleb had left over a thousand pounds, and I remembered him sitting in the cowshed, counting a roll of notes, saying, 'I'll show 'em one day. I'm worth more'n they'm be. They'll know one day.'

Now the day was here, the pity was that Caleb couldn't witness his triumph. All those years of saving and going without, making sixpence here, a shilling there. Caleb had brought up a family on a weekly wage of twenty-one shillings. Except for the last few years of his working life his wage had never exceeded thirty-two or three shillings a week. And yet he left a thousand pounds.

With Caleb's death, it seemed to me, as if an era had passed. Perhaps it had.

CHAPTER FIFTEEN

Sweet o' the year

My father visited us occasionally, usually on a Sunday afternoon, my mother much less often. Uncle George brought them in the van and when Mother accompanied them Father crouched in the back. My mother didn't like travelling in the van, she complained about the smell of pigs. Molly did not altogether welcome her visits, not because of anything she said, the dearth of speech being more of an offence. No, what Molly resented was my mother's insistence on entering every room, upstairs and downstairs, each time she came. Prying, Molly called it, but she managed, successfully I think, to hide her annoyance during my mother's presence.

We were surprised, but pleased, when Aunt Aggie came. She hadn't been to Perrygrove before. Uncle George brought her in the van.

'I would have come before, but I haven't felt up to it, but now the weather's better I said to George that I'd like to come over and see you, and so here I am. It was kind of George to bring me, wasn't it? Sam couldn't come, he's feeling a bit poorly. I mustn't stop long, I must get back to him, I don't like to leave him for long. That's why I hardly ever go to town now, and George misses his bit of fish; I always used to get him some fish when I went. I don't get about much, hardly step outside the door, so it's such a treat to come and see you both today. What a big house! Oh, such a big house!'

Aunt Aggie looked about, inspecting one room and then another and all the while saying, 'What a big house, and what a lot of work.'

As we walked back to the kitchen, Aunt Aggie and Molly in front, Uncle George and I a few yards behind, she said, 'Sam would have come, but he couldn't.'

'Not much odds,' muttered Uncle George to me.

Everyone goes into the kitchen in our house; as with most farmhouses, the kitchen is *the* room. Uncle George and I sat down at the table and Aunt Aggie managed to usher Molly into a corner. She looked at Molly anxiously; her face showing distress, thin hands fluttering, long black frock almost touching the floor, 'I don't know how you manage my dear,' she said solicitously. 'This house must be a lot of work, and no help. And you help outside, I don't know how you do it.' Aunt Aggie's voice dropped to a whisper, I could scarcely hear her: 'You must be careful, you know. You haven't any news, my dear, have you?' Her voice barely discernible now, Molly looked puzzled and shook her head. 'No signs of a little one?' asked Aunt Aggie, all eyes.

Again Molly shook her head.

'You must take care when there is, my dear.'

Uncle George had been busily filling his pipe and lighting it. 'What be them two on about?' he asked, when the pipe was going well.

Aunt Aggie became secretive, turning her back on Uncle George and on me. Later, Molly told me she'd been informed by Aunt Aggie that I was the last of the family and that anyone would have thought a big woman like that Ethel would have had more than one. That she, Aggie, would have liked lots of children but was unable to have any. That Sam would have liked children, that Sam adored children. I told Molly that I'd heard Sam say on many occasions, 'Kids?—I do hate 'em.'

'Just like women, gettin' in a huddle and whisperin'' grumbled Uncle George. 'Let's go an' see the pigs.'

'George, George, we must be off,' exclaimed Aunt Aggie. 'I must get back to my poor old Sam.'

Alfred Tucker came to kill the pig. And Uncle George came to supervise. As the trembling, squealing, protesting animal was dragged out of the sty, I would have gladly called the whole thing off, but for the presence of Alfred and Uncle George, the hardened and experienced slaughterers of pigs.

'You chaps get 'em too fat,' grumbled Alfred, cutting open the carcass.

'Poppycock,' snorted Uncle George. 'You can't have 'em too fat. I never reckon a pig's fit for killin' 'til he can hardly turn in the cot. Fat bacon, hot or cold, you can't better it.'

'They don't like 'em too fat today, George,' said Alfred, head down, busy with the entrails.

'Who don't?' demanded Uncle George.

'A lot of people.'

'Well I bain't a lot of people an' I likes 'em fat. That shop

172

bacon's no bottle, it ain't got enough fat to fry itself. Fat bacon an' a mug o' cider, who could want better'n that?'

Alfred gave the chitterlings a preliminary cleaning and then Molly took charge of them. She would clean and turn them every day for a week, in salt and water, turning them on a stick. The pig killing provided Molly with plenty of work. The liver, lights, heart and melt to be turned into faggots; the leaf to be rendered into lard and the head to be made into brawn. 'Nothin' wasted in a pig, except the squeal,' observed Uncle George.

When Alfred Tucker returned three days later to cut up the pig, he said, 'Your Uncle's all out of date with pigs, his ways are no good. I'll show everybody the way with pigs. High class breedin' stock, scientific feedin' and housin', all the modern methods, the best of everythin'. Just as you'd expect from Alfred Tucker.'

Molly, overhearing this, said tartly, 'Some of the meat you've been sending us, Mr. Tucker, hasn't been very good.'

'I do send you the best of what I've got,' Alfred grunted, looking rather perturbed. 'It aint' no fault o' mine that it ain't as good as it should be, it ain't any of my choosin', I gotta have what they do send me. But', continued Alfred, brightening up and returning more to his usual bombastic self, 'once these regulations and restrictions an' all be over, it'll be different. When I can buy my own animals—an' only the best, the very best'll be good enough for me—you'll find a difference.'

'I hope it'll be soon then', replied Molly, 'because we could hardly eat that beef—if it was beef—you sent to us last week.'

'An' so do I. An' so do I,' said Alfred.

Alfred cut up the six joints of pig meat; and the flitches and hams which I would cure. 'Your missus don't half speak her mind,' he said just before he left.

I planted some plum trees in the orchard. Raspberries, gooseberries, black currants and rhubarb in the garden. Mrs Gymble brought half-a-dozen of Fred's roses and a rosemary bush, saying in an aside to Molly, 'When there's rosemary in the garden, the woman's the boss.' Mr Darcy brought more rose bushes; a couple of cabbage roses, another called Village Maid and a Rosa Mundi. 'I haven't much opinion of these modern roses,' he told us, 'they've got no scent.'

'There,' said Molly, while I planted these, 'you grumbled about what my garden would cost and we're being given most of the plants. Plants you'd have a job to buy, anyway.'

The sword-like leaves of the daffodil bulbs she'd planted last autumn were piercing the earth's crust. 'Spring will soon be here,' said Molly.

But the spring was a long time coming. The mild wet days of February were followed by some cold harsh days in March. A north-easterly wind swept across Perrygrove, buffeting against the house and buildings. There was no refuge from it; in the fields it tore right through us, cattle hunched their backs and tried to find some shelter from the bare hedges. The wind lashed round the buildings with a cutting intensity; slates rattled and occasionally one came hurtling down. At night when we were in the house we heard the wind howling and whining outside.

'It's a lazy wind,' shouted Mrs Gymble, bowling along on her bicycle, 'it goes right through you. My Fred's blue with the cold when he gets—' A sudden extra strong veering gust took her unawares. Her bicycle wobbled, came almost to a stop; Mrs Gymble was caught, leaning at a precarious angle. For a moment I thought she'd topple off, but she was made of stronger stuff than even I'd supposed. With head down, elbows raised and legs straining, she overcame the wind and rode on.

The rooks were trying to rebuild their nests in the tall elms, but the wind made their task difficult. They clung to the windswept trees and when they attempted to fly they were blown hither and thither with their wings outstretched. The blades of the autumn sown wheat hugged the ground, shrivelling and turning blue. The water-logged land began to dry out, but all the earth looked hard and unkind.

The wind ceased as suddenly as it had started; the rooks were able to continue with their building, the weather became warmer. Celandines began to speckle the roadside banks. And in the sheltered bottoms of the hedges primroses appeared and the blue of periwinkles was discernible, the birds began to sing, winter was losing its grip.

It was possible to walk in the fields without that depressing, squelching sound. The ploughed land began to crumble, by kicking the furrow ridges a little dust could be raised. I was eager to start the spring cultivations. Mr Wrenn counselled patience. Mr Darcy said, 'There's no power in the sun yet.' Mr Saggamore, whom we hadn't seen for some time, called. 'I've been laid up with a touch of the screws,' he explained. 'You'll do no good yet, underneath the ground is still wet and unkind. If you get on it now you'll have the devil's job to get a tilth.'

Molly oiled the lawn mower and started pushing it across the unkempt lawn. The smell of the grass, the first real smell of spring, increased my impatience. But at last the time came when tractor and cultivator could wisely be taken on the ploughed land. I spent days cultivating, harrowing and rolling the ground, harrowing and rolling again, in preparation for the sowing of oats and barley. In the hedges blackthorn began to bloom, shyly at first and then in a blaze of white, the blackthorn having the whitest of all blossom.

'When the blackthorn blossoms white,
Sow barley day and night.'

There wasn't an hour to lose. Molly milked the cows in

175

the afternoon so that I could remain in the fields. At mid-day she brought me food and a flask of coffee and while I sat under the hedge to eat and drink, she drove the tractor. She'd only recently learned to drive, you will remember that at Willow Farm, where she'd worked, they'd only had horses. It is, as I discovered, a mistake for a husband to teach his wife to drive.

Molly listened attentively enough to my instructions, but we reached the stage when she thought she could drive and I was equally convinced that she couldn't. The tractor would bound forward dangerously. 'How dare you swear at me,' Molly would say; when alarmed, I would shout. Once she had the steering wheel clutched in her hands she believed she was mistress of the situation when obviously she wasn't. Well, trained horses will not plunge into hedges and ditches but a tractor will if not controlled. With horses, everything is before the driver, but with tractors the implement is behind; it means a constant turning of the head.

'Look behind you,' I had to yell to Molly. 'Quick, look where you're going.'

'How can I look where I'm going if you keep making me look behind?' cried Molly in exasperation. 'How do you expect me to do anything right if you keep confusing me? How can I learn if you keep stopping me?'

We'd passed that stage. Molly could now handle the tractor tolerably well, but as I sat under the hedge I still watched her progress towards the ditch with trepidation.

After the corn was planted we took part of a day off—our lives were governed by the milking and the feeding of stock—and went to a furniture sale. The house was still sparsely furnished and every weekend Molly scrutinised the local weekly paper for announcements of forthcoming sales. We'd been to a few sales already, buying a chair at one, a table, a roll of carpet at another. In Molly's monthly magazine there was a column about furniture, and the woman who wrote it—unlike us was always finding 'the most exquisite piece of furniture for a song' at auction sales.

Sometimes we'd see Josh Matthews at these sales. Josh in a 'pork-pie' hat and with a bundle of notes—Josh always dealt in notes if he could. 'Anythin' pertickler you're lookin' for?' he would ask, raising his hat to Molly; Josh being excessively polite on these occasions. 'If you'll let me know, I'll get it for you.' We thanked him and shook our heads, murmuring 'no, no.' Josh's commission or profit was fierce; we preferred to do our own looking and buying.

We bid cautiously, shillings if not pennies had to be considered and we often returned home empty handed. But this time we bought a tea-set for more money than we could afford. It was frivolous, we could have managed very well without it. But Molly and I had a weakness for china. The sun was shining, the milk cheque had arrived that morning. We bought the set, experiencing that delicious feeling of being extravagant—a feeling which can only be enjoyed to the full when you can't afford it—enhanced by a tinge of guilt. We wrapped up the pieces in old newspapers and stowed them carefully in our bicycle baskets. 'Oh,' Molly exclaimed on our way home, every time we rode over a bump in the road, 'I hope our china's all right.'

A sound of brakes, skidding wheels, crashing gears; I saw Mr Darcy emerging from his motor. Molly was already out of the house and talking to him when I approached. 'My sister Agatha has sent me,' he said. We had to wait a minute or two to find out why his sister Agatha had sent him. Eventually he spoke again, 'My sister Agatha has some ducklings for sale. She'd wondered if you'd care to buy some.'

'Oh yes,' said Molly immediately; too immediately, breaking all the rules of buying. The correct procedure, even in the matter of buying a few ducks, is to be non-committal when suddenly faced with an offer to sell. But not Molly; without waiting for me to give an opinion—and in the circumstances, there was only one I could have given—she ordered three dozen and it was agreed that she should collect them that very evening.

Mr Darcy left with a crash of gears and a roaring engine, narrowly avoiding Mr Saggamore. Molly had disappeared, no doubt to arrange accommodation for the ducklings.

'Was that old Darcy?' enquired Mr Saggamore, knowing very well that it was. 'A decent old chap, but never very businesslike.' No, I thought, and didn't need to be if he'd many customers like his last. 'Too easy going,' continued Mr Saggamore. 'His chaps used to rule him, always asking them whether this or that should be done. That way's no good; you want to give men orders, not ask 'em, you've got to show who's master.'

'His sister's got some ducks for sale. Molly's having some.'

He flung up his hands in mock horror. 'Oh begod, you want to watch that. Women will fill the place up with poultry if you give 'em a chance. It don't cost 'em a penny for food and they pocket the money. And once women have a bit of money of their own they start to get independent. Then it's all up, you've got to show 'em who's master, it don't do to let women get the upper hand. Anyway, I hate poultry. Hens scrattin' all over the place, muckin' up your barns and in your feed bins; ducks quackin' everywhere. But geese be the worst, you just can't keep 'em from the back door or anywhere. Great heaps of dung on the concrete and flagstones, they've a fascination for geese.'

Just then, the geese ambled round the corner and made straight for us with outstretched necks. 'Get back, y' buggers,' said Mr Saggamore, waving his thumbstick. 'Get back y' buggers,' as the gander hissed and still came on.

The thumbstick caught the side of the gander's neck, 'Serve y' right, y' vicious sod, I hope that gives you a headache for a week.' The geese retreated and stood in a huddle in front of the house. 'There, look at the dirty varmints, pooping right by the house. I'd get them from here if I was you and a bit quick too, the quicker the better,' he said and threatened them with his stick.

Molly appeared, possibly to see what the geese were cackling about. 'Mr Saggamore's just been saying ...' I started, but Mr Saggamore interrupted me.

'Good morning, good morning, I was just passing and dropped in to see how you were.'

'Yes, I told him about the ducks and he said ...' Again Mr Saggamore cut in.

'A bit of poultry's very useful to a woman. Provides her with a bit of pocket money.'

When Molly left I questioned him about this sudden about-face and received this reply. 'Never upset a woman. Women are very funny creatures when they are upset.'

Molly's ducklings soon settled into their new home. They ate ravenously, their whole bodies quivering with ecstasy as their little brown beaks eagerly shovelled up the wet mash in the troughs. Webbed feet paddled in the mash and sloshed in the shallow tray of water. Their constant squeaks became a familiar sound. Day by day we could see those tiny animated bundles of tawny fluff growing bigger.

I also went in for poultry, buying one hundred and fifty eight week-old pullets. I had them in range shelters out in the meadow, intending to put them in deep litter sheds just before they started to lay. Once poultry had been the perquisite of the farmer's wife who fed them from her husband's corn bins. Smallholders had also kept poultry, hens, ducks, geese, turkeys; but farmers proper had scorned them. The inter-war years had altered their opinion; often it had been the wife's poultry money that had been the means of providing the small necessities during the bad years. Some farmers had started keeping laying birds in folding units before the war. Nowadays, many a farmer had laying hens in deep litter; in old cart sheds, stables and haylofts. Deep litter hens weren't much work; their eggs were clean and the hens laid well in the warmth of the sheds. And the monthly cheques from the packing station were a welcome addition to the farmer's income. Perhaps the biggest advantage of all was that in the deep litter houses the birds were safe from the fox; none of that trailing out at dusk to shut the fowls up.

'I just called to say Bill will be over tomorrow,' said Mr Saggamore. Bill Lugg was coming to help me for a few days with some fencing.

Molly took Mr Saggamore to see her garden. 'Looks very nice,' he said. 'You've put in a lot of work here. It all looks very nice now, but wait until the summer when the weeds start to grow, it'll be a very different story then. Weeds grow all the time, but it ain't 'til June that they really gets goin''.'

Molly looked a bit dismayed, but even more so when Mr Saggamore asked about her ducks.

'They've all gone,' she said.

'Gone? What d'you mean, gone?' he asked.

'One morning when I went to them, they'd all vanished without a trace.'

Molly had been in tears on that morning. There wasn't any sign of feathers, blood, or a leg or a head of a duckling. There was no damage to the pen; it wasn't a fox who'd broken in and stolen them. We searched everywhere: in the garden, under the woodpile, around buildings, in the

orchard, in clumps of nettles, but no ducks. Mrs Gymble
had said, 'Somebody's stolen them; there's them as can't
keep their thieving hands off anything.'

'That's rats,' said Mr. Saggamore. 'Rats be devils after
young ducks, they'll take 'em and never leave a mark. You
should have fixed some fine wire mesh under the pen.'

Leaving Molly, Mr Saggamore and I went to inspect my
corn crops. 'You want to get this field of barley sprayed or
the charlock'll smother it. Go an' see Tommy Henwood an'
get him to do it,' advised Mr Saggamore.

Just as he was leaving, car door open and one leg inside,
he asked where Molly was. I followed him to the house,
Molly met him at the porch door and I heard him say, 'Have
Miss Darcy got any more ducks?'

Molly said she thought so.

'Right,' said Mr Saggamore, 'you go and get another lot
an' I'll foot the bill.'

On Bill's first day with us, we asked about his courting.
Bill's face lit up.

'Olive an' me be gettin' on right dandy,' he said, looking
proud and a trifle self-satisfied. 'Aye, us be.' He lit another
cigarette and grinned for a few seconds before saying, 'I
meets 'er in The Queen's Yud. I told 'ee 'er'd come and 'er
do.' Bill's grin widened and his eyes shone. 'I do buy 'er a
port an' lemon or two, 'er do knock 'em back a treat, aye 'er
do. Then I take 'er back to'er wum. 'Er don't say a lot 'er
don't, but I never did like chopsy women. 'Er suits me, aye
'er do. Some Saturdays we do go to the pictures, aye us do.'
Bill paused to let that sink in; I don't suppose Bill had been
to the cinema half a dozen times in his life before he'd met
Olive. 'Aye, we do go to the pictures, we do,' repeated Bill,
obviously impressed. Then slowly, 'I don't care for 'em
much, but Olive loves the pictures, aye 'er do, 'er do love

'em. So arter we bin in thur for about twenty minutes—
that's enough pictures for me—I leave 'er there an' goo out
and have a drink. I might 'ave dree or fower, then I goo an'
stand outside the picture 'ouse 'til 'er do come out. Then we
catches the last buz an' I takes 'er wum, aye I do.'

A couple of days later, Bill asked Molly how wide a
double bed should be. Molly told him about four feet six.
Bill thought about this for a while before saying, 'I bought
one from Josh Matthews. 'E let me 'ave'n chup, but—' Bill
paused and looked a bit worried before saying, 'I don't know
as 'e's quite as wide as that.' His brow cleared and he said,
'But I don't aim 'im's far off it, not as you'd notice.'

When Bill was ready to leave that night he seemed a bit
fidgety. Instead of jumping on his bicycle in his usual
manner and shouting, 'so-long, then', he mooned about with
the bicycle, trying the brakes, twisting the saddle and feeling
the tyres. Then suddenly, he said, 'I'm takin' Olive wum wi'
I tonight, aye I be. I'll show 'er the bed first an' then I'll ask
'er to marry me, aye I ull.' With that, he jumped on the
bicycle and sped off with his head down.

Next morning, Bill did not volunteer any news, even hints
from Molly and me did not encourage him to give any
information. 'Do you think something's gone wrong?' Molly
said to me. 'No, I shouldn't think so, Bill seems quite
cheerful this morning,' I replied. 'Well, if he hasn't
said anything by dinner time, I'm going to ask him,' Molly
said.

Bill said nothing about the events of the night before,
neither did he mention Olive all morning. At dinner time
Molly broached the subject.

'Did Olive go home with you last night, Bill?'

'Oh, ah,' replied Bill, 'I took 'er to my wum. Aye I did.'

'Well,' said Molly—Molly is impetuous like that, she
doesn't believe in beating about the bush—'What happened?'

182

'I took 'er an' showed 'er the bed, aye I did,' muttered Bill, in a matter of fact way.

'Yes?' prompted Molly.

'An' I asked 'er to marry me,' replied Bill.

'And what did she say?' asked Molly.

'Oh, 'er said the bed's too small, that's what 'er said. That bed ain't big enough for the two on us, 'er said. I byunt agoin' to marry you, that bed's too small,' answered Bill—and grinned.

CHAPTER SIXTEEN

Good hay hath no fellow—but ill weeds grow apace

At breakfast, I said to Molly, 'It's the first day of the Show today.'

Last year we had gone to the County Show and walked what seemed like endless miles of railway sleepers until we were footsore and weary. Even the short turf seemed hard and unyielding, so different from the familiar pastures of Suttridge. If I had been wearing heavy boots my feet would not have ached so much, but I wasn't. And we were deafened by machinery; it seemed that the merchants vied with one another on who could produce the most noise from their exhibitions.

That was last year. On this day in mid June I started

184

mowing the first field for hay. I cut the first swath round the field without mishap. It's something of an adventure the first time round; you never knew what you, or rather the mowing machine might find, especially if you've never mown the field before. It can all seem perfectly harmless when the grass is short, when you're walking or chain harrowing in April. But in June, when the grass is tall, it's quite different, and if there are any pitfalls which you fail to see, stumps, holes, obstacles of all kinds, the mower is sure to find them—though not usually before damage has been done.

The hydraulically attached mowing machine worked quietly and quickly—so different from the noisy and cumbersome machine I'd first used at Suttridge. Soon I'd been round the field half a dozen times and the corners had become sharp, and I had to lift the mowing machine and turn back into the standing grass. Just a touch of the lever by my side lifted the machine unlike the old mower when you had to stretch and tug at a handle.

I was cutting the back swath when Mr and Mrs Saggamore came by. Mr Saggamore pulled up and, getting out of the car, he leaned over its roof and hailed me. 'Well,' he said, after a few minutes chat, 'we must be on our way. We're off to the Show. I wasn't none too pertickler about goin', but the missus here was keen to go.'

He moved as if to get back into the car, but the farmer and curiosity got the better of him and he walked round the car. Scrambling up the bank and clutching at a sapling for support, he looked over the hedge. 'Nice crop you've got there,' he remarked, screwing his eyes against the sun and studying the field. 'But it's young and sappy, it'll take some drying. And you want to watch that fire-leaf in it. Still,' he gazed skywards, 'if this weather continues you'll be all right. I've a damned good mind to slip back home and tell Jack to get our tack out and make a start.'

'There's only bread and cheese,' said Molly, when I went

back to the house at mid-day. 'I was getting on so well in the garden that I forgot the time; and besides, I don't want to spend time cooking when there's so much to do outside. I hope you don't mind.'

'Mr Saggamore came by this morning,' I said, 'I've started mowing before him. He said he thought he'd turn back and tell Jack to start.'

There would be a good many more like him. Those who hadn't started, even those who'd had no intention of starting for several days, would, when on their way to the Show, see other mowing machines at work and would wish they'd started. And if they didn't turn back they'd have their machines at work tomorrow morning.

I finished mowing the field that evening; Molly was still working in the garden. 'Hullo,' she said, looking up from her kneeling position, and brushing hair from her face with the back of her hand, 'I've almost finished.' As I stood in the garden with the sun going down, I could smell the newly cut grass and see the cows in the meadow. The mist was rising and the willow trees a shadowy outline. 'We're going to have a fine spell,' I said.

'Good hay, sweet hay, hath no fellow.' As true now as when Shakespeare wrote it. But the making of hay can be a very hell. Bad hay is always more expensive to make than good hay, due to the extra labour involved. It all depends on the weather.

We were lucky with the weather for haymaking. Tommy Henwood came and baled it. Diminutive Tommy on his huge new tractor, 'Like a tom-tit on a pump handle,' said Mr Saggamore.

Tommy was all right; a pleasant enough fellow so long as he wasn't upset. And at this time of year he was worried; everyone wanted their baling done at the same time. When his machinery broke down, Tommy became rather nasty, too, or as he said, 'I gets agitated.' His protruding eyes would blaze, his sallow face would perform a rapid variety of grimaces. and his feet would stamp, while his arms pummelled the air. In one field he had trouble with the knotters; it meant a trail of untied bales, frequent stops and adjustments. Tommy became 'agitated'. At last, after a long delay, Tommy managed to get the knotters working properly and was able to continue with the baling; and I stacked the bales in groups of six.

Then Josh came stumping into the field, scowling. He ignored me and made straight for Tommy. 'Hey!' he shouted, waving Tommy to a standstill. 'You was supposed to be at my place at half past fower and here 'tis bloody near six. What's the meanin' on't?' demanded Josh belligerently. Tommy explained about the delay. 'I'll be with you within an hour,' he said.

'What's the good o' that? Come on now, it'll be too late then,' replied Josh, still shouting.

'I can't leave this,' said Tommy, 'I must finish this first.'

'My hay'll be clean spoilt. Come at once. Come at once, I tell you!' shouted Josh.

'You're makin' me agitated,' said Tommy and started driving forward. 'I'll be at your place as soon as I can.'

'Oh!' exclaimed Josh, hastily jumping out of the tractor's way, 'It's like that, is it?' He strode angrily away, shouting over his shoulder, 'Sod the lot of you!'

Uncle George came to help get the bales in, bringing Reuben and Colonel with him. Uncle George wasn't much help, but Reuben and Colonel and I managed with Molly driving the tractor. Reuben stacked the bales in the barn. He was given that job because—well, Uncle George gave him the job, saying: 'They be like bricks, Reuben, an' you be a bricklayer.' All might have been well if it had been left at that, but Uncle George would keep interfering. 'Not like that, Reuben. Lor' bless the chap, ain't you got any notion at all? Put this 'un t'other way round. No, not like that, turn'un round.'

Reuben put up with these instructions and counter-instructions for some time, but at last, driven to exasperation, he said, 'Who's doin' this job, George? Thee or me?'

'You bist a quick tempered little fella, Reuben. I was only tryin' to help. Get on with it then, but don't blame me if the baggers d' all fall down.'

Sometimes bales did fall down, some mornings we'd find a heap of them that had tumbled to the ground during the night.

'Thur, thur, what did I tell you?' Uncle George would keep saying. Until Reuben said, 'You shut yer chops, George.'

Some evenings Fred Gymble would come and help us. Uncle George, observing the brawny Fred handling the bales with ease and assurance, pronounced Fred, 'a bloody good chap'. And when Colonel flung a bale which accidentally knocked Uncle George down, he called him, 'a bloody nogman'.

When we went out to the field to gather bales Molly often drove the tractor for us. 'Hold tight', I would say to the one on the trailer, 'hold tight, very tight.' Molly's driving had a touch of Mr Darcy's; she was apt to release the clutch quickly and to brake suddenly.

I came to my last field of hay. Victor Lewis was working in his field on the other side of the hedge. He'd abandoned his greasy old trilby and was wearing a straw hat. We were both turning hay when we stopped and talked over the hedge.

'I've been to see the landlord,' Victor said, 'to ask him if he'd transfer the tenancy to me. Father's retired really and it seemed a sensible thing to do, I thought. And Father thought so. But the landlord wouldn't give any definite answer. He didn't say no, mind. But he didn't say yes, either. Father says there's no need to worry, that of course he'll let the farm to me. Father says our family have rented it for years, grandfather, great-grandfather, there's allus bin Lewis's at our place. Father keeps sayin' there's no need to worry, but I don't know so much. If there's no need to worry, why didn't the landlord say yes, there and then?'

We'd hoed the rows of kale with a horse-hoe just before haymaking. The kale plants were thick in the row, we'd leave them like that. The idea was, the kale would soon grow and smother any weeds, possibly one more horse-hoeing after haymaking would be needed and that would be that, the kale would be growing well and able to look after itself. That was the idea. We'd planted the kale late, after several cultivations and intervals to allow the weed seeds to germinate and subsequent lighter cultivations to kill the seedlings without stirring up fresh weed seeds from below. It was all so well planned, so easy and foolproof, there'd be hardly any hoeing, just a couple of times with the horse-hoe, no hand hoeing.

I'd hardly given the kale a thought during haymaking; we'd been too busy anyway, the weather had been good and we'd given all our attention to the hay. Now the hay was safely gathered, I returned to the kale. It was difficult to see, it was there right enough, but dwarfed by charlock. During our absence the kale hadn't grown much, but the charlock had. The kale beneath the charlock was blue and stunted and we couldn't spray because kale and charlock both belong to the same family and what would kill one would kill the other. The mass of weeds fouled the hoe blades and we had to resort to hand hoes. Molly and I spent hours hacking away at the weeds, days and nights, weekdays and Sundays. Both charlock and mayweed had an acrid odour. Our arms ached, our backs ached, almost to breaking point. We hated that charlock and mayweed with a painful intensity.

Mrs Gymble came bowling by on her bicycle—the field was by the road, which only made it worse. Everyone, we thought, must be talking about 'that mess at Perrygrove'. Mrs Gymble slowed up and rose from the saddle, putting one foot to the ground while the bicycle was still in motion. She slid to a stop and said, 'My Fred's finished haymaking at his place, he'll come and give you a hand at nights and weekends, I'm sure. Fred's always ready to help out. Some take advantage of him, he's so good natured y'know. He'd help anybody, Fred would.'

Fred did come and give us a hand, but it was still slow work; the charlock was getting higher each day. Even with the hand hoes it was difficult to make much of a job, we had to give them up too and start pulling the charlock by hand. And the kale didn't grow either.

'One year's seeding, seven years' weedin',' grumbled Fred. 'And charlock's a booger, it'll lie dormant in the ground for years and then when it gets the chance up it'll come, whoosh! I 'ates bloody charlock. I 'ates all durned weeds. Them combines are multiplatin' 'em. There ain't enough chaps on the land today. You can't farm without plenty of labour.' Fred, Molly and I pulled with grim determination. Our arms, shoulders and backs became stiffer and ached more than ever. Especially Molly's and mine, we were at it all day; at least Fred had a respite during the day. He need not have come at all, but most nights he did. Our hands were stained green and the stink of mayweed and charlock became worse.

Josh came and looked over the hedge. 'I'd plough the bloody lot in, I would,' he said.

'We won't let it byut us,' said stolid Fred. 'Why dussent

jump over the hedge and gi'e us a hand? Thee ain't got anythin' better to do.'

Josh began to edge away, 'I've got a bit of business to attend to.'

At last we'd pulled most of the weeds, enough to give the kale a chance. I walked up and down the rows, dropping nitro-chalk along them from a bucket on my arm, bags of nitro-chalk stationed at intervals along the headland. When some rain had washed the fertiliser in perhaps the kale would pick up; at the moment it was still blue and stunted, miserable looking. Fred came one evening and helped to do the last few rows. Molly was visiting Mrs Clutterbuck and when Fred and I had finished we went to The Queen's Head.

It was a warm evening, but Podsnap was still wearing his cap, thick cardigan and breeches. 'Missus, Missus. Customers,' he shouted.

Mrs Podsnap lolloped in, still making that peculiar noise, half singing, half humming. 'Yes? What would you like?' she asked, planting her bare, sharp, bony elbows on the counter and using her hands to prop her head. 'Two big pints,' replied Fred. Off she lolloped and returned with two pints of beer, one in each hand held up high and of course she couldn't lollop now for fear of spilling them. I gave her a ten shilling note and she lolloped off for change. There was a till in the bar but she also kept a slate and chalk in the back room and every transaction had to be laboriously worked out on the slate.

''Ow you gettin' on with that charlock, then?' asked Josh, lounging in a corner. We told him we'd finished. 'Oh, there now, an' me thinkin' about givin' you a 'and termorrer, as I've nothin' pertickler on.'

'I'll bet you was,' said Fred, wiping froth from his lips with the back of his hand.

Podsnap was playing quoits and in high good humour

because he was winning. 'I'm on form tonight,' he cackled. 'I'm allus good, but tonight I'm bloody good. Nobody can beat the old man, the old man can play, ha, ha, tit-ta, tit-ta.'

Alfred Tucker walked in with a butcher's basket in the crook of his arm. 'Missus, Missus. Butcher!' shouted Podsnap. Mrs Podsnap appeared in a few seconds with a pint of beer which she handed to Alfred. She craned her neck to peer into the basket which Alfred had placed on the counter, and then, without saying a word, took the basket away.

The talk turned to early potatoes; one said Epicure was the best variety, another said Arran Pilot, a third said Sharpes Express. 'Arran Pilot's the best,' said Podsnap with an air of authority.

'I can't grow 'em in my garden,' said Josh.

'You don't try very bloody hard,' said Alfred.

'I like Home Guard,' said Fred.

'Ay, they be good 'uns,' said Podsnap.

Alfred Tucker turned towards Fred. 'You was in the Home Guard, wasn't you, Fred?' he asked.

'Ah.'

'Yes, when you was on parade, you was on parade, if your lot was like our lot, Fred. When you was on parade you was on parade,' declared Alfred in a loud voice.

'Ah.'

'Yes, when you was on parade, you was on parade,' repeated Alfred, louder still.

'From what I saw of your lot, Alf,' said Josh, 'they was mostly on parade outside The Lion; queuein' up, waitin' for it to open. No wonder beer was so scarce durin' the war.'

Mrs Tunney was standing in the doorway staring at me. She was a widow, and during the war and for a few years afterwards, she'd been porter at the railway siding where I used to take loads of plums and sugar beet. She had, as Jack would remark, 'seen a fair few summers and winters—and by the look of her a lot more winters than summers'. She stood staring hard at me, her black, coarse, unruly hair, now streaked with grey, tumbling over her swarthy face. Her gaudy, tawdry clothes were stained and dusty and her thick stockings were twisted and full of holes. But for all that Mrs Tunney had an air about her. She made a sudden dive towards me, crying, 'It's you! It's you!' She flung her arms round my neck and hugged me, then releasing me, said, 'It's a damn bloody long time since I've seen you. How are you, kid?'

Podsnap glared at me, but said nothing. I knew he didn't like having Mrs Tunney in the bar, but he'd got her now, and I decided to ignore his glowering face and the way he kept chucking his chin to show his displeasure. Instead, I bought Mrs Tunney a pint of stout, and taking a good swig, she said, 'That's damn bloody good on you, kid. I'll buy you a bugger in a minute.' Then lowering her voice. 'D'you get in here much?' I shook my head and she said, 'No, nor me. Old Poddy's too damn bloody miserable for me. I like a place where it's a bit jolly, a bit of music and singin' y'know.'

Podsnap was having an argument with Josh. 'He can't hear us, kid, he's as deaf as a coot,' said Mrs Tunney. Suddenly, bending her head towards me, she laughed and said, 'I remember one night, during the war, some Yanks came in here and they saw that pianner in the other room, an' one of 'em started playin' it. The others started to sing an' dance and one of 'em caught hold of me and twirled me round. Old Poddy started shoutin', "Hey, hey, you can't do that in here", and one of them Yanks caught hold of him and twirled him round. "Join in, old timer", they shouted to him. "Sing up, old timer". Old Poddy couldn't do anythin' about it and round and round the place they swung him, them ol' whiskers of his flyin'. And round and round I went with this big American boy. "That's the way, Ma", they all shouted. Oh, I never enjoyed myself so much. They gave me packets of fags and sweets, they bought me drink. I sat on the counter here and sang, "I wouldn't leave my little wooden hut for you". Old Poddy didn't like it, but he couldn't do a damn bloody thing. Every time he tried to, these Yanks started dancin' him round again. I could have died, I was so happy. Lovely boys, they was.

'And then they said, "We'll take you home, Ma," and off I went in their jeep. Oh, they were wonderful boys, those Yanks.'

'I'll have a game with you, Elijah,' shouted Alfred. 'I'll take on the champion.'

'You'll never beat me, Alfred,' said Podsnap, picking up the quoits.

'I'll risk it,' said Alfred, "tis only a game.'

'I'm in tip-top form to-night. I'm allus good, but tonight I'm unbeatable, ha, ha, ha,' cackled Podsnap. Podsnap soon stopped cackling when it was obvious that he was losing. He lapsed into sullen silence.

'Another game?' asked Alfred, after he'd won.

Podsnap gathered up the quoits and said, 'I'm not playin' no more tonight.' He went behind the bar and put the quoits in a cupboard and said, 'Nor nobody else ain't playin' tonight.'

The flower and vegetable gardens were both knee deep in weeds. We'd neglected the garden during haymaking and during the long hard battle with the charlock in the kale. And now we saw, instead of a garden, a wilderness of weeds. Bindweed was choking Molly's roses, lavender, rosemary and other shrubs. The pinks couldn't be seen, nor many of the other plants, only the hollyhocks towered above the smothering weeds. There was a profusion of sow thistles, dandelions and grass, nettles were re-establishing themselves —and to think how carefully we'd forked out their yellow roots last autumn, or so we thought. All those back-breaking hours of Molly's had come to this.

And the vegetable garden presented the same sorry sight; except that there, fat-hen outnumbered the sow-thistles, hiding the rows of peas, carrots, beetroot and lettuce. Bindweed had climbed up the runner bean sticks and had twisted round the sprouts and round the soft fruit bushes. Docks, brown with seed, even the hated charlock was there.

We'd been too optimistic, too ambitious. We should have concentrated on smaller areas and tamed them before attempting the whole garden. But haymaking plays havoc with the best of farm gardens. Instead of the little respite before harvest, we bent our backs or got on our knees and tried to restore some order.

We were both hard at work in the flower garden one afternoon, when we heard a bang and clatter. A few moments later Mrs Gymble strode into the garden. 'I've a couple of hours to spare, want any help?' she asked. She was soon busy in her accustomed manner, full of gusto. 'A helpin' hand's worth a ton of sympathy, I always say. I said to my Fred last night, you gave them a hand in the kale and I'll go and give them a hand in the garden.'

A few evenings later, when I came into the house, I found Molly on her knees in the kitchen. At first I thought she'd hurt herself or suddenly been taken ill, and then I saw that she was bending over a cat that was lapping milk from a saucer.

'Oh,' she said, looking up at me, 'Mrs Gymble's just been here and brought this cat. She said it was a stray that had been hanging round her place for some days—in fact I think she did mention it while she was helping in the garden. She said she didn't want it and would we like it. And when I saw it I couldn't say no. Look at it, isn't it a beautiful black cat?'

It was indeed a beautiful black cat; it also looked very well fed for a stray. Indeed, the more I looked at it, the more I thought it resembled that paragon of cats which Mrs Gymble had told me of some time ago.

CHAPTER SEVENTEEN

Full of the year

'I'm not staying a minute,' said Miss James. 'I was only passing, I'm off to see that Josh Matthews, I'm on to him like a dog to a rabbit. I'm going to jolly well make him mend his ways. He can say, Yes Miss James, No Miss James, and keep smiling and then do nothing. I'm just in the mood for him this morning, I've had a jolly good breakfast and now I'm going to jolly well make him sit up. No, no, I won't stop for a cup of tea this morning, thank you very much. I want to catch that scamp before he clears off, he won't be expecting me yet. But I'll just have a look in your dairy as long as I'm here.

'Oh, dear, dear, dear,' she said, looking at the utensils in the dairy, 'you've got milkstone on the cooler and the container and the buckets.' She was examining the clusters hanging on the wall, putting a finger inside the liners. 'And your rubbers need de-fatting.' She gave me a sharp look, 'Do you do de-fatting?'

I told her that I did not. 'It's a wonder you haven't had trouble during the hot weather. I know, I know, it's no good telling you to do these things, it's far better if I come and show you. What about next Tuesday afternoon?'

It was agreed that Miss James and I would remove the milkstone from the metal utensils and de-fat the rubber parts next Tuesday. Miss James would arrive at two o'clock sharp to give us plenty of time to finish before milking. 'I shall be coming through Oldbury, I'll stop and get the necessary chemicals from the chemist there. I'll pay him and then you can pay me. Now I must fly, I mustn't let that scamp give me the slip.'

'I didn't pay the chemist,' Miss James told me on the following Tuesday, 'I thought it would be better if you paid him yourself. He said it was all right.' She put a bottle and tin in the dairy, put a smock on, and pushing the sleeves above her elbows said, 'Let's get straight to work.'

She wore rubber gloves when using the acid to get rid of the milkstone. On her instructions I pulled the milking units to pieces, completely to pieces, separating the metal parts to treat them for milkstone; the rubbers for the de-fatting process. On Mr Wrenn's advice, I'd bought a different machine from the one I'd used at Suttridge, it had more bits and pieces; the liners had to be assembled with the aid of a special tool with which metal rings were inserted to form the one end. I hadn't mastered the knack, and once a week when I took the machine apart I had difficulty in reforming the liners; metal rings shot off the special tool and fled round the dairy, especially when the rubber liners were wet. But today, although the liners were wet, I had Miss James to help.

Miss James scrubbed and scrubbed at the cooler, in and around the corrugations that the milk flowed over. Some milkstone was removed, but more remained. 'Now you have a turn at the cooler,' she said. I scrubbed, to little effect. 'It takes time,' said Miss James. 'You'll have to have another go at it in a few days time.' She watched me for a minute, 'You mustn't have the acid too strong, or it'll ruin the surface. Now, we'll have a turn at the buckets.' We were more successful with them; time was getting on, there was all of the machine to reassemble, all those fiddling rings. Still, it would be better today; Miss James would have the knack, maybe I'd learn a thing or two.

'I went to a young farmer the other day', she said, while we were scrubbing the rubber parts, 'and helped him. I said to him, you want to see that man of yours gives them a good rinse with cold water, before scrubbing them in hot water, instead of rushing off to breakfast. Of course he hadn't got a man, I knew that. He was like you, did it all himself. But I thought it was nicer putting it like that, and now I'm saying the same to you. Make sure your man gives it a good rinse with cold water. Don't skimp that just because you want your breakfast.'

We placed the scrubbed parts in cold water containing hypochloride; how lavish Miss James was with the water. We heated more in the portable gas boiler. Miss James left the cold tap running to waste, there'd be a lot of water pumping to do later. Everything scrubbed and rinsed at last; all that remained now was to put it all together again, but with the old girl's help it wouldn't take long.

Miss James straightened her back and wiped her hands on the roller towel hanging on the wall. 'There', she said, 'that's done. Now, I won't hinder you while you put it all back together again, I'll go in the house and have a nice cup of tea and a chat with your wife!'

We cut the oats with a binder, and the barley later, mainly because corn stored better in the stack. We were keeping the oats for the cattle and the barley for the pigs. And the oat straw would be of a better feeding quality harvested this way. 'Good oat straw is better than bad hay,' said Mr Saggamore.

This coming winter we should have plenty of bedding straw, barley and wheat straw. We would be able to have cattle and pigs in straw up to their bellies, the way animals should be littered. They looked better and did better; they were comfortable with plenty of straw under them and there'd be plenty of dung made. You can't farm without dung and you can't make dung without animals and straw; that was Mr Saggamore's creed and mine as well. Unfortunately, specialised farming has ruined this excellent maxim. Some farms have no straw and too many animals, resulting in slurry and worry. Other farms have no animals and plenty of straw, resulting in the burning of straw.

While Tommy Henwood and his man cut the oats, Molly and I stooked the sheaves. Molly's mother and father were staying with us at the time and her father was keen to help. It took him a bit of time to get the knack of stooking, but what he lacked in skill, he tried to compensate with hard work. He was enthusiastic, rushing about and grabbing sheaves. 'Steady on,' we said. 'Let's get on,' he cried, no doubt thinking us a pair of sluggards. Unlike us he worked with bared arms. 'You'd be better off with your arms covered,' we told him, but he ignored our advice.

As the day went on he began to drag his feet and lag behind, although he tried valiantly to keep up with us. He'd scoffed when we'd told him to wear his heaviest shoes, he'd bustled when we'd told him to go steady, he'd ignored us when we'd told him that the straw would make his arms sore. Now he was footsore and weary, his arms were red, scratched and bleeding. Yet he kept on, wouldn't admit his mistakes.

'Father, hadn't you better rest awhile?' said Molly.

'No, no, I'm all right, don't worry about me,' he puffed and wiped the sweat from his face.

Rabbits began to bolt as the area of standing corn got smaller. Molly and I caught three and every now and then Tommy's man would leap from the binder and give chase. 'What sport! What sport!' cried Father-in-law. He too would have liked to give chase, but the effort was more than he could manage. Almost at the end, I saw a rabbit run from the corn; saw it stand, confused, not knowing where to go in this strange world of stubble and sheaves. It crept under a sheaf close to Father-in-law. 'Quick,' I shouted, 'fall on that sheaf right by you, there's a rabbit under it.' He flopped on the sheaf—by this time it was almost all he could do. 'Now, work your hands underneath and catch it.' After groping under the sheaf, he rose painfully to his feet holding the rabbit. 'One for the pot! One for the pot!' he cried, triumphantly. But before I could take the struggling rabbit from him it escaped. 'Oh, dear,' he exclaimed, his triumph turning to dejection.

A fox slunk out of the corn and made for the hedge. It seemed in no great hurry, there was almost insolence in the way it made its escape. 'That's the first live fox I've ever seen,' Molly's father told me excitedly, 'except for the one in Bristol Zoo.'

That night as he was going to bed, he remarked, 'I shall sleep well tonight.' But not once did he admit that he was almost exhausted, neither did he complain about his feet and arms.

Two mornings later he went for a walk. 'I met a most interesting man at The Queen's Head,' he told us on his return. 'He's a farmer, and from his conversation I gather that he must have quite a large farm, though you'd never have thought so from his appearance. He was most untidily attired, but obviously he was a most hard working man, a true son of the soil.'

Who could it have been? Roger Warren was the only large farmer who visited The Queen's Head, as far as I knew. And I'd never seen him dressed untidily; besides, he was of a taciturn nature, it was unlikely that he'd have much to say to a stranger. 'A most engaging character,' said Father-in-law. 'He farms quite close to the Queens' Head. He has a large flock of sheep, and a considerable number of milking cows.'

That ruled out Roger Warren, he lived some distance away and had no milking herd. Molly's father was obviously impressed by this farmer, and continued, 'A man of considerable experience. I learnt a lot from my morning's meeting. Very sociable, a most agreeable man. A great knowledge of horses, cattle, sheep and crops.' What did he look like, we asked.

'A real countryman. A hardworking farmer. Down to earth. One who could turn his hand to anything, a man who loved all classes of stock, except pigs—he didn't seem to like pigs.'

'Did he have wicked little eyes?' I asked quickly.

'He had sharp eyes. Very sharp eyes.'

'Josh!' exclaimed Molly and I together.

Molly's parents had gone before it was time to cart and stack the oats. On the morning we started, Jack appeared. 'Hullo,' he said, standing holding his bicycle. 'I've come to give you a hand. The boss said you'd be gettin' them oats in, so as we'd nothin' much on for a day or two, I asked if I could have two or three days of me holidays so's I could come and give you a hand.'

I thanked him and explained that we'd hoped to have Uncle George later in the day. Colonel and Reuben had also said they'd come, but according to Uncle George, 'they've gone missin'. Them two be gone to flickuts. I don't know whatever's come over 'em.'

'Ah, them two, they don't like a lot of work—not reg'lar. They never did,' said Jack. 'But I like a bit of harvestin' with sheaves. Combinin's all right, it's quick an' all that, an' none o' that dirty old dreshin' arter, but it ain't like sheaves.'

Jack and I pitched sheaves to Molly on the wagon. Jack unloaded and Molly passed the sheaves to me as I built the stack in the barn. 'Like old times, ain't it?' remarked Jack, and smiled. 'Only wants the boss an' old Bill here.'

'How is Bill?' I asked, we hadn't seen him since the day after Olive Cox had refused to marry him.

'Oho!' exclaimed Jack, smiling broadly. 'He's gettin' married on Saturday.'

'No!'

'Yes, he's goin' to the registry office in town this next Saturday.'

'We thought it was all off between him and Olive.'

'Oh, he ain't marryin' Olive.'

'Who then?'

'Mrs Tunney. Didn't you know? Old Bill's full of it, talked about nothin' else lately. I should've thought you'd have been bound to have heard.'

'I'm surprised.'

'So'm I. So's the boss. We never thought Bill'd ever get married. The boss keeps sayin' to me, "D'you think he's gone off his head or summat, Jack?" Oh, it's awful, you dursen't take yer eyes off old Bill for long now, you don't know what he'll be doin' next. Talk about didows, 'tis didows all the time now, with Bill. The boss gets really angry with him at times and keeps sayin'—"He's gone right off his head, Jack. I don't know what we shall do with him, Jack."—And Gritton's that nasty. Oh, there's summat goin' on at our place all the time now, 'tis a proper circus.'

'We must give Bill a wedding present.' said Molly.

'Fancy old Bill getting married.'

'Ah,' said Jack. 'I'll be glad when 'tis all over. I hope old Bill 'ull calm down then and stop some of them didows. The boss gets that angry, but it don't have any effect now. Bill just keeps grinnin'.'

'I wonder what we could give them?' Molly said. 'We won't be able to get anything before the wedding, we'll have to give them something after their honeymoon.'

'They bain't havin' no honeymoon,' said Jack. 'Old Bill 'ull be back at work on Monday.'

Tommy Henwood combined the wheat and baled the straw, the wheat was only a moderate crop. 'I reckon your ground's a bit deficient,' said Mr Saggamore. 'You should have had a better crop than that. I shouldn't be surprised if that ain't what's causing the trouble with your cattle, deficiency of the soil or summat. I'd get it analysed if I were you. Barnard used too much nitrogen to my mind. You want some sheep folded over the ground, there's nothin' like sheep.'

When we'd finished corn harvest, Molly said, 'Let's take Bill's present tonight. It's Sunday, he's sure to be in.'

Bill opened the door to us; his face registered puzzlement, surprise and then pleasure. 'Come on in,' he said. We stepped straight into a small cluttered and untidy room. Molly handed him the present, which he unwrapped. 'Oh, that's nice,' he said, rather embarrassed. 'That's nice.' He held the tablecloth which we had given him and muttered, 'That's nice, 'er 'ull like that.'

'Congratulations on your marriage, Bill,' I said.

Bill looked more embarrassed and said, hesitantly, 'I byunt married, no I byunt.'

'But Jack told us that you were marrying Mrs Tunney.'

'So I was,' replied Bill.

'Oh dear,' said Molly softly, sensing something had gone wrong.

'Well, I be married,' said Bill, brightening up, 'but I byunt married.'

Mr Saggamore must have been right after all, poor old Bill must have gone off his head—or summat, probably summat.

'But you must know if you're married or not,' said Molly, gently.

'Well,' said Bill, bolder now, 'I byunt married an' I be married, aye I be.' He grinned, relaxed now. 'It's like this yer. Me an' Mrs Tunney was goin' to git married, aye us was. We went off to town to do it, me an' Mrs Tunney an' our Grit, an' a couple of others. An' we got there too soon, aye us did. An' our Grit says, "Let's go an' 'ave a drink, better'n 'angin' about," an' 'e takes us off to a pub 'e knows, aye 'im do. An' 'e buys a drink all round, an' I buys a drink all round, an' Mrs Tunney buys a drink all round, an' t'others buy drinks all round, aye 'em did. An' that's 'ow it went on, all very nice, an' all of us clean forgot about the weddin', aye us did. Then one of us remembers, but arter us got round to the office, they be closed, ay 'em be. An' our Grit says, "It's no good 'angin' about." "No," says Mrs Tunney, "I was never a one for mopin' about." "Let's go to the Dogs," said our Grit. "Good idea," says Mrs Tunney, an' t'others, an' me, aye I did. So us all went to the Dogs, an' arter us went an' 'ad some fish and chips an' a drink or two.'

'Oh, what a shame,' said Molly.

'No 'twasn't,' replied Bill, 'we all 'ad a good time, an' we brought some beer back 'ere an' 'ad a bit of a party, me an' Mrs Tunney, an' our Grit an' t'other two an' a few more we'd collected up. An' Mrs Tunney never made no fuss about that bed bein' too small, no 'er didn't.'

'Well, you can go and get married another day,' Molly said.

'No. Mrs Tunney an' me ain't goin' to bother. It don't seem worth it now, we'm all right as we be, aye us be.'

'You don't still call her Mrs Tunney, do you, Bill?' I asked.

'No. 'Er name's Margaret. I call 'er Margaret, but sometimes I forgets and calls 'er Mrs Tunney, aye I do.'

Mrs Tunney came in through a door at the back of the room. On seeing us she stopped, mouth agape, hands held high. 'It's you, kid!' she gasped, taken aback, and then hugged me before saying, 'I've only just got in, never thought to see you. Well what a blasted surprise. And this is your wife?'

Bill gave her the tablecloth. 'Oh, that's bloody good on you, kid. Thanks to both of you. I'll treasure that. Bill's my chap now, what do you think about that?'

Later she said, 'You wasn't more'n a boy when you used to bring them plums to the station, an' now you're married. D'you remember when I had that piano accordion? They wanted me to go on Workers Playtime, but I couldn't leave Daddy, he was very ill, even then.'—Daddy was her husband, Mr Tunney—'And then when Daddy died, I was lonely. And Bill, he was lonely. There's a terrible lot of loneliness in the world. It's a damn bloody thing, loneliness. But Bill an' me's all right now, we've got each other, we're lucky. Damn bloody lucky. You're damn bloody lucky. We're all damn bloody lucky. Let's all 'ave a drink, eh?'

We had a good crop of plums, but so did every farm. The market prices were low, the contract price was also low—if you could get a contract. Unlike milk, meat, eggs, corn and sugar beet, there was no guaranteed price and market for plums. The new men in farming talked of grubbing their orchards, some had already done so. The older men, the local men just grumbled and hoped next year would be better, some of them saying, 'Taking one year with another, plums have always paid the rent.' Plum pickers were difficult to get and the ones we did get created further difficulties. They demanded more money, although prices were so low. They quarrelled among themselves, about who had the best trees, about ladders and baskets, about the number of boxes they'd picked. And they were unreliable, they asked for their money each night. If I paid them there was no telling if they'd return, if I refused to pay, they sulked.

I couldn't help remembering with affection those plum picking days at Suttridge with the miners. They never quarrelled with anyone, they were totally reliable and worked hard from dawn to dusk; often sleeping in a hay loft so that they could make an early start. There were no surplus plums either, in those days, their price and destination were controlled by the authorities.

After plum picking I laid a field down to grass, ploughed the stubbles and an old pasture that the Agricultural Committee had drained. And soon it was Michaelmas again.

'We've been at Perrygrove twelve months today,' I said, as I helped Molly to wash the tea things. Molly was going to see the Clutterbucks and we'd had tea slightly earlier than usual.

I waved goodbye as she rode along the lane and then went to feed the pigs. The weaner trade was down and so I'd kept them. In a way I wished I'd let them go. Josh was right, 'pigs do yut too much'.

Later I went to see the in-calf heifers, those I'd bought last autumn at Mr Clutterbuck's sale, they would be calving in a fortnight's time. The heifers clustered round me, sleek and rotund, udders already well formed and tight. They sniffed my clothes in what seemed to be half fear and half faith, muzzles pink and exuding a sweet smelling bovine breath.

I walked past the alders and willows which lined the

banks of the chuckling stream and went to see the young stock. By this time dusk was falling, I could hear Molly in the orchard, calling the ducks. 'The second year's harder than the first, lad,' Mr Wrenn had told me recently. We were still short of money, our cattle were still afflicted occasionally with mysterious ailments, we still had the twice daily pumping of water. But Molly and I were young and healthy, in love with life and with each other.

When I went into the kitchen Molly already had a cloth on the table. The oil lamp was lit, casting a rosy glow on knives, plates and cups, clean gleaming. Molly, hair dishevelled and face slightly flushed from her bicycle ride and from the exercise known as 'shutting the ducks up', was putting cheese and home-baked bread on the table. Soon we would sit down and while we ate we would talk about the Clutterbucks, and perhaps some news she'd heard.

'How are the Clutterbucks?' I asked a few moments later, when we were sitting at the table. Strange that Molly hadn't volunteered information. Usually on returning home, even when she'd been no further than the Post Office, or away for only half an hour, she was bursting with chat.

'I haven't seen them tonight,' she said, pouring coffee.

'But I thought that's where you went.'

'Oh, no. Not tonight.'

'But, that's what you told me?'

'Oh, did I?' This calm, rather indifferent reply was also a little irritating.

'Well, if you didn't go to the Clutterbucks, where did you go?'

'I went to see Dr Higgins.'

'You're not ill, are you?' Sudden, irrational fear came over me. 'You haven't said anything to me. What did the doctor say?'

'He told me that I'm a perfectly normal healthy girl and there should be nothing to worry about.'

'But, why, why?'

'Oh, you great silly,' said Molly, smiling broadly, 'Can't you guess? Can't you see what I'm trying to tell you ... I'm going to have a baby'.

ROSEACRE

ELIZABETH HOUSE